The

Kitchen
Witch

Your Complete Guide to
CREATING A MAGICAL KITCHEN
WITH NATURAL INGREDIENTS,
SACRED RITUALS, AND SPELLWORK

SKYE ALEXANDER

Foreword by Arin Murphy–Hiscock,
Author of *The Green Witch*

ADAMS MEDIA
NEW YORK   LONDON   TORONTO   SYDNEY   NEW DELHI

▲adamsmedia

Adams Media
An Imprint of Simon & Schuster, Inc.
100 Technology Center Drive
Stoughton, Massachusetts 02072

First Adams Media hardcover edition July 2023

ADAMS MEDIA and colophon are registered trademarks of Simon & Schuster, Inc.

For information about special discounts for bulk purchases, please contact Simon & Schuster Special Sales at 1-866-506-1949 or business@simonandschuster.com.

The Simon & Schuster Speakers Bureau can bring authors to your live event. For more information or to book an event, contact the Simon & Schuster Speakers Bureau at 1-866-248-3049 or visit our website at www.simonspeakers.com.

Interior design by Colleen Cunningham
Interior illustrations by Claudia Wolf
Interior images © 123RF

Manufactured in the United States of America

1 2023

Library of Congress Cataloging-in-Publication Data
Names: Alexander, Skye, author.
Title: The kitchen witch / Skye Alexander, foreword by Arin Murphy-Hiscock, author of The Green Witch.
Description: First Adams Media hardcover edition. | Stoughton, Massachusetts: Adams Media, 2023. | Series: House witch | Includes index.
Identifiers: LCCN 2023004994 | ISBN 9781507220887 (hc) | ISBN 9781507220894 (ebook)
Subjects: LCSH: Witchcraft. | Magic. | Handicraft. | Kitchens--Miscellanea.
Classification: LCC BF1566 .A5467 2023 | DDC 133.4/3--dc23/eng/20230307
LC record available at https://lccn.loc.gov/2023004994

ISBN 978-1-5072-2088-7
ISBN 978-1-5072-2089-4 (ebook)

Contains material adapted from the following titles published by Adams Media, an Imprint of Simon & Schuster, Inc.: The Modern Guide to Witchcraft by Skye Alexander, copyright © 2014, ISBN 978-1-4405-8002-4, The Modern Witchcraft Guide to Fairies by Skye Alexander, copyright © 2021, ISBN 978-1-5072-1591-3, and The Modern Witchcraft Spell Book by Skye Alexander, copyright © 2015, ISBN 978-1-4405-8923-2.

Contents

Chapter 5
Inviting Others Into Your Practice / 87

Chapter 6
Kitchen Witchery for the Holidays / 104

Part 3
An Encyclopedia of Magical Edibles / 123

Part 4

Common Spells, Charms, and Rituals for Kitchen Witches / 203

Candle Spells

Witches' Brews

Botanical Baths

Crafty Spells

Foreword

KITCHEN WITCHCRAFT IS THE MEETING place of hearth-based spirituality and plant-based practice with a focus on food. I'm very much a green witch and a hearth witch, but despite this background, kitchen witchcraft is somehow not an area in which I feel very secure.

I suspect there is a disconnect between the kitchen representing magical transformation, and a conflation of cooking successfully and self-worth. I don't feel confident about cooking, and am always surprised when something I make turns out well. This is completely at odds with how I approach magical work. It's also at odds with how much I enjoy baking. Whatever the root of my difficulties with identifying what I do as kitchen witchcraft, they exist, and I'm constantly working through them.

Fortunately for both you and me, Skye is very comfortable in the kitchen witch zone. Skye has vast experience in so many different areas of metaphysics and nature-based spirituality, so what she brings to the field of kitchen witchcraft is rich and confident. Her writing style is direct, clear, and grounded. Her work is always a joy for me to read.

The kitchen is a place of transformation, communication, and community. It's a magical place, so it only makes sense to engage in magical activity there. Skye looks at how to approach witchcraft via the kitchen witch lens, and discusses topics like sabbats, correspondences, energy management, and tools in the light of a kitchen witch's focus and activity. Using basic supplies that can be found in supermarkets, she provides a terrific cross section of examples to experiment with.

My favorite part of this book is the extensive section on foods and ingredients, featuring magical energies and associations, as well as some cultural and historical uses. When every part of your daily life involves engaging with magic, even the sandwich you make and the smoothie you sip can be designed for specific goals, and supported with intentionally selected ingredients.

Whether you identify as a kitchen witch, green witch, hearth or house witch, or something else, *The Kitchen Witch* will help expand your practice by suggesting ways in which your everyday activity can be enhanced with magic. If you haven't previously felt confident about kitchen magic, be prepared for inspiration and new ideas to play with as you go through this book.

Arin Murphy-Hiscock
Author of *The Green Witch*

Introduction

BOTH THE HEARTH AND FOOD satisfy fundamental needs in us all—warmth and sustenance, comfort and fulfillment. It is no surprise that great importance and power have been placed in both these domestic areas throughout the ages. The kitchen witch unites the power of the hearth, the bounty of nature, and the spirituality of the home to find balance and peace. It is a path that follows simple methods to provide powerful results.

Kitchen witches weave their magic into their everyday domestic tasks and use the magical properties of herbs and foods to infuse their cooking with certain energies to meet their magical goals. Unlike some forms of magic, kitchen witchery doesn't require a lot of fancy tools, elaborate rituals, or esoteric knowledge. It's not something you do only on the sabbats—you practice it *every day*, in your own special way. But don't let the apparent simplicity and homeyness of kitchen witchcraft fool you. It's meaningful and compelling because it's an integral, natural part of your life.

With *The Kitchen Witch*, you'll learn what's unique about this form of witchcraft and what it means to be a kitchen witch. You'll read about the history and folklore of kitchen witches and about the goddesses and gods in many cultures who preside over hearth and home. You'll also find an encyclopedia of over one hundred common plant-based, natural ingredients along with their magical properties, to help you determine which ones will best aid in producing the results you seek. If you're already walking the path of the witch, you'll discover ways to bring familiar parts of the craft into your daily domestic life. Plus, you'll find ideas, techniques, rituals, and methods for expanding your practice as a witch.

Magic isn't something you *do*, magic is what you *are*. When you embrace the way of the kitchen witch, you realize that magic is everywhere, in everything, waiting to be discovered. It's your birthright, something that's natural and available to everyone. So turn to your hearth, your cooking tools, and your favorite ingredients and get started on your path to kitchen witchery.

Part 1

What Is Kitchen Witchery?

Magic isn't something witches do, it's what they are. They don't put aside their magic when they go to their day jobs or drive the kids to school or wash the dishes. For witches, every facet of their lives is imbued with magic and each act is a mystical one. The mundane and the magical are entwined, not separate. And nowhere is this more apparent than in kitchen witchcraft.

Long before many of the paths magic workers tread today existed, kitchen witches plied their craft in their homes and communities throughout the world. Kitchen witches dispense with a lot of ceremonial formality in favor of practical, down-to-earth, everyday engagement with the natural world.

In the chapters that follow, you will explore what kitchen witchery is and how it differs from other similar types of witchcraft, like green witchery and house witchery. You'll discover how kitchen witches use the magic properties of foods and spices to infuse their cooking with specific energies and how to treat your kitchen like the sacred space it is. Finally, you'll learn about the history of hearth magic and some deities and magical beings from around the globe who are tied to kitchen witchery and the hearth.

Chapter 1

What Does It Mean to Be a Kitchen Witch?

KITCHEN WITCHES FIND THE MAGIC in the everyday. They caringly and mindfully prepare food for their loved ones and use the magic energies of food and spices to empower their food with their magical objectives. They view their kitchens as sacred spaces and treat them with respect and reverence. And they put positive energy and intention into their household duties. What some may view as a burdensome chore, kitchen witches view as an opportunity to weave magic into their day.

In this chapter, you'll learn about the path of kitchen witches and how they differentiate from other types of witches. You'll also take a look at what things are important to kitchen witches and how they weave their magic into their homes and hearths.

The Path of the Kitchen Witch

Kitchen witches, also sometimes called cottage witches, create most of their magic in the home and hearth. Magic is woven into their domestic tasks, which they do with intention and purpose, from gardening to cooking to laundry. They use common kitchen implements as their magical tools, know the magical properties of herbs and foods, and put intention and magic into their meals.

The kitchen is a sacred place for this type of witch, and they pay close attention to the ingredients—and the quality of those ingredients—that they use in their cooking. They research both the nutritional properties of their ingredients and their magical properties as well. They use that information to get ideas about dishes, beverages, and remedies to prepare either for themselves or their loved ones based on things they might be going through—both healthwise and emotionally.

Location Is Not a Limit Stereotypically, people envision kitchen witches in charming cottages in the woods, communing with nature and growing all their own food, but that is not necessarily the case. In reality kitchen witches live all over, from suburbs to cities to the countryside as well. Where you live has no bearing on what kind of witch you want to be.

Kitchen witches may do some or all of the following things in their practice:

- Eat whole foods that are unprocessed and grown from the earth
- Grow their own foods and herbs or try to buy these products from local sources
- Try to live a sustainable lifestyle
- Consider their kitchens sacred spaces and treat them as such, with ritual cleansings and cleanings as well as more mundane organizing
- Research the magical properties of herbs and spices and learn how to transfer these qualities to the foods they cook

- Brew teas and tinctures from herbs
- Place crystals around their homes for peaceful energy

In short, kitchen witches can be people from any place or background who believe in the magical powers of the home and food and use those powers to influence their own magic. They know that everything carries energy and that they can use that energy and infuse it with their own personal energy toward their intent.

Once you assume the mantle of the kitchen witch, you'll begin to see food, cooking, and eating in a whole new way. Breakfast is no longer a doughnut and cup of coffee you gobble down as you rush to the office—it's a way to welcome the new day and all its possibilities. Lunch becomes a salute to the sun and the day's apex, during which you honor your work, your talents, and the gifts you offer to the world. At supper, especially if you share the meal with family or friends, you give thanks for the many blessings you've received during the day. Each meal—from grocery shopping to preparation to consumption, even cleanup—nourishes both body and soul.

How Kitchen Witchcraft Is Unique

Anyone can be a kitchen witch, regardless of the magical path he or she follows. You can be a Wiccan, Dianic, Gardnerian, hereditary, eclectic, or chaos witch—or something else—and also engage in kitchen witchcraft. One doesn't necessarily rule out another, although some are more similar, and admittedly it can get confusing.

What's the difference between kitchen witches, green witches, and house witches? Naturally, you'll notice some overlap. Kitchen witches operate within their homes, just as house witches do, and consider their living spaces to be sacred. Green witches use herbs and other plants to work magic, and so do kitchen witches. You may also hear kitchen witches referred to as hearth witches and green witches called hedge witches. So let's take a quick look at some of the particulars in these categories, without getting too specific. You can find many good books that cover various traditions and styles of witchcraft in more detail than this book has space for.

Witches, Wizards, Sorcerers, and Magicians The words *witch*, *wizard*, and *sorcerer* can be used for people of any gender. *Wizard* derives from a term meaning "wise," and *sorcerer* means "witch" or "diviner." The word *magician* is also appropriate for all genders and for witches of all stripes. Depending on the cultural setting, the term *magician* can describe people adept in astrology, sorcery, divination, spell casting, and/or other magical arts. Don't call a male witch a *warlock*, however. That's an insult—the word means "oath breaker" or "liar."

HOUSE WITCHES

House witches practice home-based spirituality. Their homes exist at the core of their spiritual paths; they're sacred spaces imbued with energy, power, and love. The domicile in which a house witch lives is more than a building that provides shelter, comfort, and safety. It's a holy place, a sanctuary, a temple where every chair, table, rug, bed, and lamp—every ordinary object—resonates with the witch's unique energy.

A house witch's home is a haven for those who dwell there as well as for visitors. It may be luxurious or modest, a cottage in the country or an apartment in the heart of a city. It may include "witchy" items—goddess figurines, an ornate chalice, a crystal ball—or not. But regardless of its physical features or locale, when you enter the home of a house witch, you instantly feel welcome and nurtured, even though you may not understand exactly why.

> **A House Witch** "While other spiritual paths often look *beyond* the home to focus on the natural world, the house witch creates a solid and supportive place to work from—a literal (and magical) home base."
> —Arin Murphy-Hiscock, *The House Witch*

The house witch uses magic to create a harmonious environment by dispersing disruptive energies and encouraging peaceful, happy ones. She's a priestess who fills the space with reverence—she may even invite beloved deities, spirit guardians, or honored ancestors to join her there. He's a guardian who guides the flow of energy, balancing yin and yang forces by using ritual, intuition, wisdom, and the power of intention. In short, the home is an expression of the witch's spirituality, and everything that takes place there supports that path.

GREEN WITCHES

As you might expect, green witches practice nature-based magic and spirituality. They work with herbs, flowers, essential oils, and other botanicals for healing, nutrition, spellcraft, and more. They're the folks whose gardens grow lush and abundant, who prefer natural herbal substances for healing and personal care, and who eschew pesticides and toxic chemicals in every area of their lives.

The green witch has more than a green thumb, though. Green witches have a reverence for and an affinity with the natural world and attempt to live in harmony with it. They don't just exist on this earth, they understand they are *of* the earth—nurtured, supported, and integrally entwined with this planet. They have an intimate relationship with Mother Earth and all living things that share the world with them. As Arin Murphy-Hiscock writes in her book *The Green Witch*, the witch "is aware of how the energy of nature flows through her life and environment."

Green witches don't necessarily live in the country or the woods, as one might think (and as they often did in earlier times). These days they're more likely to live in suburbs or cities. Nor do they live apart from other people and the world at large—your mechanic or hairdresser or insurance agent might be a green witch. In some instances a green witch may learn skills from a parent, grandparent, or other relative, but witchcraft doesn't have to be in the person's lineage. The way of the green witch is an individual and personal one—you don't need to get a degree in agriculture or undergo formal training to walk this path. Nature itself is the green witch's teacher.

The Magic in the Everyday

Witches of many persuasions celebrate eight sabbats, or sacred holidays—Samhain, Yule, Imbolc, Ostara, Beltane, Litha, Lughnasad, and Mabon—and perform magic rituals, rites, spells, and so on during these special days. But you don't have to wait for a sabbat to do your workings. In fact, if you're a kitchen witch, you probably cast spells of some sort every day. That's one of the reasons kitchen witchery is so effective—you live your craft and bring it into all you do. Some of the things kitchen witches do to embrace everyday magic include:

- Saying a blessing before eating a meal
- Cooking with certain spices for their magical properties as well as their flavors

- Burning candles of colors that match your objective and enjoying their light while you eat supper
- Offering a cup of specially brewed tea to a guest
- Weeding the herb garden while talking to the plants
- Sweeping the floor and whisking away bad vibes in the process
- Arranging flowers (chosen for their magical properties) on the dining table

These things may seem simple—and they are—but that doesn't mean they lack power. You empower them with your will. Your energy and intentions transform ordinary actions into extraordinary ones.

Cook with Mindfulness and Intention

You've heard the expression "You are what you eat," right? For kitchen witches, this doesn't refer only to the vitamins and minerals in their food. A witch's thoughts, emotions, and intentions are just as important—maybe more. For this reason, as a kitchen witch, you practice mindfulness at every step, from choosing the food you eat to preparing it to eating it and even cleaning up afterward. Mindfulness means putting your full attention on what you're doing, being present in the moment, and focusing your mind instead of letting it wander.

For the kitchen witch, this also means monitoring your thoughts and keeping them on positive things while you're engaged in your work. That's because thoughts have power. They precede action and manifestation. And the more you think about something, the more likely you are to bring it into your life—that's what's known as the law of attraction. This is especially true when a kitchen witch is preparing a meal or an herbal remedy or a magic potion. You project your thoughts into whatever you're concocting, whether it's a soup or a love spell, and those thoughts affect the outcome.

Turn Off the TV You probably know people who watch TV while they're making breakfast or dinner. Often they watch the news, with its nonstop litany of crimes, horrible accidents, and devastating natural disasters. The disturbing thoughts and images engendered by these reports go right into these people's food and then into their bodies. Instead of allowing their health and well-being to be adversely impacted in this way, conscientious witches banish TVs from their kitchens.

Knowing this, you can consciously create the circumstances you seek by infusing your food with your intentions. Is attracting money a priority for you? Do you want to get a better job? Would you like to bring more happiness into a relationship? The first step is to set that intention and make it a priority. Then, from the moment you enter your kitchen, hold the intention in your mind. As you prepare meals, project a picture of the outcome you desire into each dish you create. As you eat, envision each bite fueling your goal as well as nourishing your body, mind, and spirit.

Nourishing Yourself and Others Is a Spiritual Act

Kitchen witches are passionate about their cooking. After all, it's an integral and important part of their lives, on many levels. They needn't be gourmet chefs—the care and enthusiasm they invest in the meals they prepare and serve to their loved ones are what matter. Food preparation takes on special meaning when you see each step of the process as working magic. When made with the right intent, even simple mac and cheese can be a magical meal.

The kitchen is a holy place for the kitchen witch, where mystical activities merge with practical ones, where transformation occurs as raw ingredients are turned into manifestations of love and life. The witch is a priestess or priest; cooking is a sacrament; the meal is a precious gift.

In short, kitchen witches concern themselves with nourishing the soul as well as the body. They pay attention to the physical properties of the food itself but also to the spirit in which each meal is created and the environment in which it is consumed. If you view the body as a temple, you'll treat it as such and do your best to respect and care for it.

Using Affirmations, Gratitude, and Blessings to Benefit Hearth and Home

Affirmations are short, simple statements that express your intentions. They direct your subconscious to fulfill your objectives. Create affirmations in the present tense, as if the conditions you desire already exist. Use only positive terms and images in your affirmations; for example, say, "I am completely and radiantly healthy in every way" instead of "I don't have any illnesses."

Affirmations are a quick and easy way to incorporate powerful words and ideas into your everyday life as a kitchen witch. You can use them in practically any situation, in connection with nearly any action. As you cook and clean, use affirmations to bless your home and loved ones. Here are some examples, although you should feel free to create your own:

- When you open the kitchen door, say, "Only health, love, and joy come through this door into this home."
- While stirring food in a pot, say, "Thanks be to all beings who contributed to this meal."

- While serving food, say, "The food I prepare and share nourishes my loved ones in body, mind, and soul."
- While sweeping, say, "All harmful, disruptive, and unbalanced energies are removed from this place."
- When you turn off the kitchen light at night, say, "Bless this kitchen and this home and keep those of us who live here safe and healthy throughout the night."

Your Kitchen Is Sacred Space

As a kitchen witch, your kitchen is your sacred space. This room is your place to work magic, whether it's a tiny galley in a high-rise apartment or a great room with all the latest sophisticated accoutrements in an elegant mansion. What does that mean to you?

Take a few minutes to remember one or more places you've been that have felt sacred—a church or temple, perhaps, or maybe a grove of old trees or a peaceful pool of water. That's the feeling you want to bring into your kitchen. Now, consider what you can do to create that feeling in your own home. Begin by thinking about the things that contributed to the feelings of love, peace, and joy in the sacred places you've visited before. How do you want to treat a place of your own that is sacred to you?

- Will you keep it clean and neat?
- Will you remove any objects that don't contribute to the ambience you desire for this space?
- Will you forbid arguments from taking place in your kitchen?
- Will certain topics, such as politics or petty gossip or what occurred in your office today, be banned from your kitchen?

- Will you play soothing music?
- Will you install artwork that represents your objectives and pleases you when you look at it?
- Will you establish rituals that, when you enter this space, help you shift your thinking from mundane to mystical?

The list is probably endless and will differ from person to person. Most likely, it will also change from time to time, as you do.

Quick Clearing Ritual Before you enter a space that you feel needs a bit of cleansing, enact this quick and easy clearing ritual. Close your eyes, take a few deep breaths, then sweep your arms in a 180-degree arc across the area several times while saying aloud, "This space is now cleansed and cleared of all harmful, disruptive, and unbalanced energies. It is filled with divine white light, healing energy, and love." While you say this, envision the entire area surrounded, suffused, and purified by white light and sense it being brought into balance.

YOUR KITCHEN IS A PLACE FOR MAGIC

Nurturing and protecting home and family are primary concerns for kitchen witches—and woe be to the person who threatens their domestic harmony. The kitchen is not only their sanctuary, but the workshop where they ply their trade as well. Chapter 4 will examine ways to organize, design, and consecrate this special place in more detail. But for now, let's look at this central room in your residence that other people (and maybe you, too, until you assumed your role as a kitchen witch) only view in practical terms.

First, consider what purposes you'll assign to your kitchen. Preparing meals there is a given and a fundamental part of your role as a kitchen witch. But since antiquity, witches have performed many other tasks in their kitchens. You may choose to concoct herbal medicinal remedies here, as witches throughout history have done in their roles as healers, midwives, cunning folk, and protectors of hearth and home. You may decide to prepare magic potions, talismans and amulets, teas and witches' brews, or charms and fetishes here. Maybe you'd like to make candles and personal-care products—soaps, lotions, and so on. Your purposes will dictate how you design this magical space.

Each item in a witch's kitchen has a purpose—probably more than one, for it's likely to serve as a magic tool as well as a mundane cooking implement. The magic part might not be obvious to the untrained eye, however.

Kitchen Witchery Can Be Private Not everyone is ready to go public with their witchy ways. They may fear criticism from family and friends, or worry that their everyday work lives would suffer if their bosses and colleagues knew about their metaphysical beliefs. One of the great things about kitchen witchery is that you can practice your craft without letting everyone know. Who's going to know the broom you use to sweep the floor is a witch's besom? That goblet you use in a toast for good health looks like an ordinary glass, but *you* know it's really a magic chalice. And all those spices you sprinkle into the meals you cook? They add flavor, certainly...but maybe something more.

Preparing and Eating Food Magically

Whether you opt to eat meat, fish, or only vegetables is a personal decision. As a kitchen witch, you should prepare and consume whatever food you've chosen with mindfulness, respect, and gratitude.

EXPRESSING GRATITUDE

Many people are familiar with the practice of saying grace or some sort of blessing before they eat. This may entail thanking a god or goddess for your food and for the companions with which you share it. It may mean stating an affirmation that the meal you consume will provide nourishment for your bodies or expressing another form of acknowledgment and gratitude, instead of simply chowing down while watching TV.

Try this: Before you eat, thank everything and everyone who made it possible for you to enjoy your meal. This may include the benevolent deities who govern our world; the animals and plants that surrendered their lives for your benefit; the birds, worms, and insects that participated in the plants' growth; the earth from which the food came; the sun; the rain; the nature spirits; the farmers who raised what you are about to eat; the people who harvested it; the truckers who brought it to market; the supermarket and all the employees who made it available for you. Not only does this practice make you conscious of how much is involved in even a simple meal, it reminds you that we are all interconnected and dependent on one another for survival.

Give Back Keep the cycle of giving and receiving going by sharing your time, money, or other gifts. Donate to programs that feed the hungry. Volunteer at a local food bank or homeless shelter. Deliver food to shut-ins. Get involved in environmental organizations. As witches know, whatever you do returns to you threefold.

MEALTIME RITUALS

When you perform a ritual, you engage in a series of actions designed for a particular purpose. Rituals provide a sense of stability and continuity in your life. They also help you focus your mind and shift your thinking from one area to another. Religious rituals, for example, move you out of the mundane world and into the spiritual one. Your morning ablutions prepare you physically, mentally, and emotionally to enter the workday world; nighttime ones get you ready to sleep.

As a kitchen witch, you can choose to design rituals that celebrate meals and encourage diners to be mindful of what they eat as well as the overall experience. Your rituals will also be magical workings. When planning a ritual, first set an intention and then organize the various steps and factors so they support your goal. Let's say, for instance, you want to improve your financial well-being. Here are some things you could include in a prosperity ritual:

- Prepare a meal using ingredients associated with prosperity. (For help with this, check out Part 3 of this book.)
- Put a green or gold tablecloth on the table to symbolize money. Green also brings to mind healthy plants, and gold represents sunshine.
- Carve candles with dollar signs or other symbols that signify money and set the candles on the table. Light them just before you begin to eat.
- In the center of the table, place a vase of flowers associated with prosperity, such as daffodils or tulips.
- Lay a coin underneath each diner's plate.
- Dress for dinner, instead of "coming as you are." Wear clothing that makes you think of wealth and success, not your go-to worn-out jeans or a ratty old T-shirt.
- Ring a bell at the beginning of the meal and again at the end, to signal the start and finish of the ritual.

Changing Places Sometimes your familiar rituals can become so habitual that they limit you. Try to counter this by having each member of the family sit in a different place at each meal. This shakes up the accustomed order and enables diners to see one another from various perspectives.

- Invite one or more of your favorite deities to join you.
- Before eating, say a blessing composed to attract abundance and give thanks, as if your intention has already manifested.
- During the meal, avoid discussing unpleasant or discouraging topics. Keep it positive.

USE THE POWER OF MAGIC DAYS

Each day of the week is ruled by one of the heavenly bodies. Therefore, the day's energy and the areas of life connected with it are influenced by that particular body. As a mealtime ritual, you can tap into the qualities of each day with your magic by preparing and eating food that relates to the areas governed by the day's celestial ruler. For example, on Monday, you might focus on enhancing family relationships by including dairy products or shellfish in your diet. On Tuesday, serve spicy dishes to magically enhance vitality or libido. Here are some suggestions:

Monday ∾ Ruled by the Moom
- Areas of influence: home and family matters, fertility, creativity, intuition
- Moon-ruled foods: milk, cheese, ice cream, chicken, beef, clams, oysters, crabmeat, cucumbers, avocados, lettuce, eggs, pumpkins, turnips, watercress

Tuesday ∾ Ruled by Mars
- Areas of influence: athletic contests, competition, courage, strength, vitality, men, sex, passion
- Mars-ruled foods: chilis, garlic, onions, pepper, ginger, horseradish, lamb, mustard, radishes, bananas, carrots

Wednesday ⌁ Ruled by Mercury

- Areas of influence: communication, commerce, intellectual matters, short trips
- Mercury-ruled foods: dill, fennel, oats, corn, wheat, nuts

Thursday ⌁ Ruled by Jupiter

- Areas of influence: growth/expansion, prosperity, long-distance travel, higher education, religion/spirituality
- Jupiter-ruled foods: apricots, asparagus, berries, currants, figs, liver, rhubarb, sugar

Friday ⌁ Ruled by Venus

- Areas of influence: love, romantic and business partnerships, money, the arts, beauty, women
- Venus-ruled foods: apples, artichokes, beans, chocolate, candy, cherries, confectionary, honey, pears, peaches, pecans, potatoes, strawberries

Saturday ⌁ Ruled by Saturn

- Areas of influence: limitations, structure, responsibility, authority, tradition, endurance, stability, protection, work
- Saturn-ruled foods: barley, beets, mushrooms, parsnips, persimmons, prunes, salt, spinach, yams

Sunday ⌁ Ruled by the Sun

- Areas of influence: public image, confidence, career pursuits, health/well-being, creativity
- Sun-ruled foods: almonds, walnuts, citrus fruits, grapes, olives, rice, sunflower seeds

Using Sacred Plants

Plants are living entities, and the life force within them makes it possible for kitchen witches to use them for food, medicine, and magic. Many witches believe plants contain consciousness and intelligence too. Researchers have learned that plants communicate with each other, warning one another of insect infestation and sending signals and protective chemicals to aid their neighbors.

Other studies demonstrate that you may contribute to your plants' well-being by talking nicely and playing classical music to them. Plants also display memory and innate wisdom that enables them to develop ways to improve their lives. Authors Peter Tompkins and Christopher Bird in their bestselling book *The Secret Life of Plants* describe experiments that showed plants may even have emotional responses and the ability to recognize individual people.

Ask the Plant's Permission Before you cut or pull up a plant to use for food, healing, or spells, ask the plant's permission. If you sense it's okay to proceed, go ahead; otherwise, seek out another plant instead. Not only does this show respect for another living being, but it also invites the plant to willingly participate in your work.

SACRED WOODS

The Druids considered plants, and trees in particular, to be sacred. So do many witches. Plants not only nourish and heal us, they serve as guides and teachers for humankind. Some Indigenous people also use plants for spiritual journeying and to expand human consciousness. Thousands of years ago, the Aztecs and Maya ate psilocybin mushrooms for divination purposes, and the Lakota in North America still use peyote in ceremonies to gain insight from higher realms.

Although you'll find differing opinions about which woods were sacred to the Druids—who even created a tree alphabet called ogham—here's a list of some that usually fit into that category. Note that this list is based on trees that grow in Britain, Ireland, and parts of Europe. Elsewhere in the world, the trees native to certain regions will likely be considered sacred by the Indigenous people who live there.

Sacred Woods and Their Magical Attributes

- **Apple:** love, knowledge, beauty
- **Ash:** strength, intellect, willpower, protection, justice, balance and harmony, skill, travel, weather magic, wisdom
- **Birch:** protection, cleansing and purification; use birch twigs to make a besom
- **Cedar:** spirituality, purification, protection, wealth, career success, recognition
- **Elder:** healing, protection, prosperity
- **Hawthorn:** fertility, harmony, happiness, protection, otherworld connections
- **Hazel:** luck, fertility, protection, wisdom
- **Maple:** love, prosperity, health
- **Oak:** strength, courage, longevity, protection, good fortune; Yule logs are usually oak
- **Pine:** purification, mental clarity, healing, prosperity, protection
- **Poplar:** prosperity, communication, exorcism, banishing, purification
- **Rowan:** protection from evil, improving psychic powers, divination, healing, creativity, success, transformation

- **Willow:** love, tranquility, intuition, harmony, protection, growth, renewal, healing; willow is a favorite wood for dowsing rods
- **Yew:** witchcraft, the spirit realm, death and transformation, nature magic

COOKING ON A FIRE MADE OF SACRED WOODS

Can a kitchen witch enhance the magic and enjoyment of a meal by cooking it over a fire made of sacred woods? Absolutely. The energy, intention, reverence, and focus you bring to your workings give them their power. Add to that the innate qualities of the woods themselves, and the combination is nothing short of amazing. Especially on the sabbats, at lunar rituals, or on other dates that hold significance for you, cooking with sacred woods and then sharing your meal with family and friends can be a joyful and inspiring experience.

Ideally, you'll want to use a cauldron to prepare your magical meal. Some cauldrons have grills or racks that enable you to build a fire in the belly of the cauldron and grill meat or vegetables on top. If you prefer, you can position the cauldron over a fire (in a firepit or fireplace) and cook the meal in the cauldron.

Choose one or more woods whose associations correspond with your intentions. For example, if you want to attract prosperity, consider burning cedar or poplar in your cook fire. Ash and rowan are good choices if protection is your goal. Include as many different types of wood as you feel are necessary to accomplish your objectives. Well-dried wood burns better than green wood, so you may want to stockpile several of your favorites to use throughout the year.

On a piece of paper, write your intention. Add this to the fire. As the paper burns, envision your intention rising on the fire's sacred smoke to the heavens, where the deities will hear it, and then manifesting in the physical world.

Cook the meal you've prepared over the fire, keeping your objective in mind. The ingredients you've chosen for the meal should also represent your purpose (see Part 3 of this book to learn more about the special properties of herbs, spices, and other magical edibles). Invite your favorite deities to join you. Give thanks for the food you eat and to everyone who has helped make your meal possible. Then share the meal with loved ones, each of whom will participate in the fulfillment of your intention.

When you're finished and the cook fire has died down, collect some of the ashes and save them to use in talismans, amulets, or charms or in other magical ways.

Chapter 2

A History of Hearth Magic

KITCHEN OR HEARTH WITCHERY IS one of the oldest forms of witchcraft, and it's gaining popularity today among modern magic workers. Modern-day kitchen witches find their forebears in the village healers, herbalists, and wise folk of years long past. This chapter will explore the history of kitchen witchery and hearth magic. You'll learn about the various examples of house witches throughout history in different cultures and the deities, fairies, creatures, and spirits who have been a part of hearth magic.

A Woman's Place

Traditionally, the home and especially the kitchen have been considered the domain of women. Therefore, it's no surprise that the majority of kitchen witches in the past were female. Although that's still true today, old attitudes and divisions of labor are changing—there's no reason why men can't be powerful kitchen witches too, and indeed, many are.

Historically, herbalists, midwives, cunning folk, and witches in general tended to be women. Before the advent of allopathic medicine in the

1800s, women healers cared for the sick. They brought babies into the world. They shepherded the dead into the afterlife. They brewed curative teas, prepared salves and poultices, and cooked nourishing soups in their kitchens. They grew medicinal and magical herbs in kitchen gardens. In bygone days, people believed female witches even controlled the weather.

Weather and Witchcraft Weather played a part in the witchcraft hysteria of Salem, Massachusetts, where nineteen people (fourteen of them women) were executed as witches in 1692–1693. Beginning in 1680, Salem had experienced exceptionally cold winters that caused illness and poor harvests. When the reverend Samuel Parris's daughter Betty became sick in 1691, he pointed his finger at local "witches." In Europe, a period from the early fourteenth to the mid-nineteenth century known as the Little Ice Age coincided with the execution of tens of thousands of people, most of them women, accused of witchcraft during "the Burning Times."

Naturally, this gave them considerable power, but it also made them vulnerable to suspicion and fear. If someone fell ill after eating a meal, the woman who prepared it might be blamed for putting poison in the food. If crops failed due to inclement weather, a female witch might be held responsible and punished.

The Importance of the Hearth

Although we don't know how long people have used fire to warm themselves and cook food, archaeologists estimate we've done so for at least a million years. For the ancient Greeks, the hearth served spiritual as well as practical purposes. In addition to cooking at the hearth, people made sacrifices and offerings there to the deities, particularly to the goddess Hestia.

A town's center and marketplace often featured a communal hearth where a fire was kept burning continually, tended to by unmarried women.

The term *hearth* refers to the floor and interior part of a fireplace where a fire can be built, as well as the extended area in front of it. A hearth may be made of brick, stone, tile, or, in some cases, hard-packed earth. The term may also describe a section of masonry or other fireproof material on which a woodstove or cookstove sits. Before electricity, people gathered around the home's hearth for warmth; to cook food; to heat water for washing; to read and sew by firelight; to commune with family, friends, and neighbors. In short, the hearth fire served as the home's center of activity.

The Focus of the Kitchen The Latin word *focus* translates as "fireplace" and "hearth," but it also means "center." The hearth fire is the center and focus of kitchen witchcraft.

Our modern homes may feature fireplaces or woodstoves, but few of us cook on them today. Instead, the role of the hearth is now filled by the kitchen stove or perhaps a barbecue grill or outdoor firepit. As a kitchen witch, you still perform not only practical tasks at your "hearth," but spiritual and magical ones too.

Kitchen Witches in Fairy Tales, Folklore, and Legends

Many people were introduced to witches through fairy tales. The folklore and legends of cultures the world over offer fantastic stories of magical beings, beneficent as well as evil, who cast spells to bring good fortune or punish human beings. These witches concoct magic brews in their cauldrons, serve enchanted food, grow mysterious plants in their kitchen gardens, and preside over the harvest. However, it's good to remember that fairy tales were morality lessons and often portrayed witches in a less-than-favorable light. Here are some well-known kitchen witches from various cultures.

FRAU HOLLE

A popular kitchen witch in Germanic folklore is Frau Holle (also known as Holda or Hulda and by other spellings), who performs domestic tasks and has connections with beings in the spirit realm. In one of the Brothers Grimm's fairy tales, a girl falls into a magic well and ends up in the realm of Frau Holle. There the girl meets enchanted bread and apples that talk to her, and she becomes a household helper to the witch, who treats her well and feeds her roast meat every night.

As Christianity gained a footing in Europe, its disciples labeled pagan deities witches—with a derogatory connotation, of course. The bishop Burchard of Worms, Germany, in his *Decretum* (circa 1008–1012 C.E.), claimed Frau Holle was a demon doing the devil's work. However, the Church couldn't eradicate her from folklore, where she remains as an overseer of domestic life who helps the needy, brings snow in winter, and scares lazy children into doing their chores.

It's likely the colorful kitchen witch poppets that hang today in German and Scandinavian kitchens to bring good luck were inspired by Frau Holle. Usually fashioned to look like stereotypical old women with pointy hats who are riding or carrying brooms, kitchen witch poppets are said to keep pots from boiling over, prevent food from burning, provide safety in the kitchen, and bring happiness to the home.

What's a Poppet? Poppets are effigies that represent people in spellwork. A poppet may be made of cloth, straw, wax, wood, or another material. Don't confuse it with a doll, however. Dolls are toys; poppets are witches' magic tools.

BABA YAGA

Russian folklore gives us a strange and creepy version of the kitchen witch in the figure of Baba Yaga, whom the Brothers Grimm appropriated for the fairy tale "Hansel and Gretel." Baba Yaga uses a unique form of transportation to get around the forest: a mortar and pestle, in which she can pound herbal medicines or grind the bones of her victims. In some renditions of her tale, she rides in a witch's cauldron. She lives in the forest in a hut perched on chicken legs and surrounded by a fence made of bones. In the Grimms' telling, the witch's house is "built of bread and covered in cakes." She lures the children to her home, planning to fatten them up before she eats them—a perverse inversion of the philosophy of kitchen witchery.

Witches or Fairies? According to nineteenth-century scholar Thomas Keightley's work *The Fairy Mythology*, women "skilled in magic" (i.e., witches) were referred to as fairies in old French stories. "All those women were called fays who had to do with enchantments and charms…and knew the power and virtues of words, of stones, and of herbs."

SNOW-WHITE AND THE SEVEN DWARFS

Another well-known Grimms' fairy tale, "Little Snow-White," introduces aspects of food as magic. When Snow-White's stepmother, presented as a jealous queen and witch, wants to eliminate her competition, she orders a hunter to take the child into the forest and kill her. He's supposed to return with the girl's heart, which the queen/witch plans to eat in order to become immortal. But the hunter takes pity on Snow-White and lets her go free.

The exhausted girl comes upon a cottage in the woods and falls asleep there. When she wakes up, she discovers she's in the home of seven dwarfs. They agree to let her stay, so long as she cooks and cleans for them (is she a kitchen witch as well as a servant?). Snow-White lives with the dwarfs until her wicked stepmother discovers the girl is still alive. Disguised as an old woman, the queen gives Snow-White a poisoned apple that throws her into a deathlike sleep, until a prince wakes her with a kiss.

THE CORN MAIDENS

Various Native American legends speak of one or more corn maidens who brought precious maize to the people. In a Zuni legend, seven maidens produced corn of six different colors by sloughing off their skin, which became the kernels. However, the men of the tribe scared off the maidens (in some versions, the women were believed to be witches), who went to live in the land of summer. Each year, though, they returned in the spring to plant a new crop of corn and make sure the people were nourished.

In a Hopi legend, the Blue Corn Maiden was the best loved of the sisters for the wondrous blue corn she provided. One day the Winter Katsina, who brings cold weather to the land, captured the Blue Corn Maiden and imprisoned her in his home. The Summer Katsina found her there, and the two male deities fought. Finally, they negotiated a truce: The Blue Corn Maiden would spend half the year among her people and give them corn. For the other half of the year, she'd live with the Winter Katsina, during which time the crop would die. Obviously, the story represents the changing seasons and the ongoing cycle of life and death, and it bears similarities to the Greek myth of Demeter and Persephone.

BRITAIN'S BROWNIES

In English and Scottish folklore, magical beings known as brownies take on the least glamorous of a kitchen witch's responsibilities: cleaning and tidying the kitchen at the end of the day. Usually portrayed as little old men dressed in humble clothing, they show up and get to work after everyone else has gone to sleep. They connect themselves with particular families, like loyal servants, and some sources say brownies are spirits of deceased relatives. Legends say they're fond of bread and honey cakes, so if you want to solicit their aid, leave these treats out for them as a thank-you gift.

Deities of Hearth and Home

The myths and spiritual teachings of cultures throughout the world speak of powerful and beloved deities who govern hearth and home. These goddesses and gods are responsible for providing food for their people, presiding over the harvest, and ensuring human life on earth. Not surprisingly, they're highly revered and treated with the utmost respect. In some cases, these deities produce magical edibles that possess special qualities in addition to nourishment.

HESTIA/VESTA

Known as Hestia in Greek mythology and Vesta in Roman, this fire deity was revered in both civilizations. The Greek poet Homer called her the "chief of the goddesses," showing how important the hearth was in early communities. As mentioned earlier, the hearth served spiritual as well as practical purposes in these ancient cultures—it was the place where people not only cooked, but where they also made offerings to the deities, and primarily to this goddess, who ruled the hearth. Before the members of the household ate, they said prayers to Hestia and cast a choice piece of the meal into the fire in honor of her.

DEMETER

Hestia's sister in Greek mythology, Demeter is sometimes called the Goddess of Grain or the Corn Goddess—the name of her Roman counterpart, Ceres, is the root of our word *cereal*. She's the goddess of agriculture, who nurtures the crops and controls the harvest.

One of the best-known stories about Demeter involves another magical edible. In it, the goddess's daughter Persephone is abducted by the god Hades (who's also Demeter's brother). He whisks the girl away to the underworld to be his wife. While in captivity, Persephone makes the mistake of eating some pomegranate seeds, which prevent her from leaving and escaping the realm of Hades permanently. She's then doomed to spend part of each year in the underworld, during which time the earth sleeps and crops don't grow. Thus, the myth represents the planet's seasons of fertility and rest.

BRIGID

One of the most beloved and powerful goddesses in the Celtic pantheon, Brigid goes by many names including Lady of the Flame, Goddess of the Hearth, and Bright One. The goddess of healing, smithcraft, and poetry, Brigid presides over both the homemaker's cook fire and the metalsmith's forge. Her sabbat in the Wheel of the Year, the holiday of Imbolc (also called Candlemas), is usually celebrated from February 1–2. *Imbolc* means "in the belly" and signifies Brigid's role as a goddess of creativity.

Artists' renditions often show her stirring a great cauldron, the witch's magic tool that symbolizes the womb and the receptive, fertile nature of the Divine Feminine. As goddess of inspiration, Brigid encourages everyone, regardless of gender, to stir the inner cauldron of creativity that exists within each of us.

KAMUI-FUCHI

The Japanese goddess of the hearth is known as Kamui-Fuchi; her name means "rising fire sparks woman." She protects and oversees the home, where a fire is kept burning for her at all times. When the goddess and the family go to sleep at night, they cover her fire with ashes to protect it and prevent it from going out. According to myth, the goddess never leaves the hearth, but has other spirit helpers who report to her. In her role of presiding over domestic affairs, Kamui-Fuchi observes human actions and metes out justice for right and wrong behavior.

One legend says she descended from the heavens, another that she was born from an elm tree. In Ainu tradition, the hearth is the place where souls are held until they take on human bodies; thus, Kamui-Fuchi has a connection with procreation and reincarnation. She also serves as a liaison between earth and the heavens, enabling families to communicate via fire with their ancestors, who were believed to abide in the hearth.

KAMADO-NO-KAMI/KOJIN

In Japan, Kamado-no-Kami, also known as Kojin, is the god of the hearth, cook fire, or stove. *Kami* means "spirit." A protector spirit, Kamado-no-Kami guards the family and makes sure the fire as well as the food cooked on it are safe. *Kamado* is also a term used for a cooking pot or cauldron. In addition to presiding over the hearth and kitchen fire, the god also protects cattle and horses. Japanese families position shrines above their stoves to honor this fire deity, who prevents cooking accidents and brings good fortune. Legends also connect him with purification, particularly that which comes from fire and burning.

FREYA

Mythology tells us the Norse/Germanic goddess Freya brought light and fire to the people of Northern Europe. Her name means "lady" and is spelled in various ways, including Freija, Frøjya, and Frejya. A fiery deity, she's linked with the flames of the hearth and the forge, similar to the Irish goddess Brigid. Although usually thought of as a love goddess, she also plays a key role in warfare. Folklore says that whenever soldiers die in battle, she chooses half of the fallen men and shepherds them into the afterlife; the others are consigned to Odin's great hall in Valhalla.

WANGMU NIANGNIANG

Worshipped in China and other Asian countries, the goddess Wangmu Niangniang is known by many names including Queen Mother of the West. She's the epitome of female power and the personification of yin, the primal feminine force in the universe. The goddess lives in a palace atop Mount Kunlun in western China, where an otherworldly garden with rare peaches grows. According to mythology, the tree puts forth fruit only once every three thousand years. Anyone who eats the goddess's magic peaches at her legendary banquets becomes immortal.

THE CHINESE KITCHEN GOD

Also known as the Hearth God or the Stove God, the Kitchen God called Zao Jun, Zao Shen, or Tsao Wang in Chinese culture is one of the most popular deities. Each Chinese family has its own kitchen god, who serves as an emissary and go-between, interacting with human beings and the higher-up divinities. He's also a spirit guardian who protects the family and oversees domestic affairs.

Artists depict him with his two wives, and Chinese homes often display paper images of him above the kitchen stove. According to tradition, a family's kitchen god travels to heaven each year to give an account of his family's behavior to the Jade Emperor. To make sure he speaks sweetly, the family dabs honey on the paper lips of the kitchen god and then burns the paper to send him on his way.

BEER GODDESSES AND ALEWIVES

For thousands of years, we've been brewing and drinking beer—and for much of that time, women were right in there with the men. An ancient Sumerian song dedicated to the goddess Ninkasi—a revered kitchen deity—even contains the oldest-known instructions for making beer. The early Egyptians worshipped a beer goddess called Tenenet. Slavic myths speak of the goddess Raugutiene, the protector of beer, and Finnish legends say beer was invented by a woman named Kalevatar, who might have been a kitchen witch. During medieval and Renaissance times, brewing beer and ale was a regular part of a woman's domestic work throughout Europe when lack of sanitation made it safer to drink fermented beverages than water.

According to Addison Nugent, writing for *Atlas Obscura*, medieval Englishwomen who brewed and sold beer, known as brewsters or alewives, "had several means of identifying themselves and promoting their businesses. They wore tall hats to stand out on crowded streets. To signify that their homes or taverns sold ale, they would place broomsticks—a symbol of domestic trade—outside of the door. Cats often scurried around the brewsters' bubbling cauldrons, killing the mice that liked to feast on the grains used for ale."

The medieval church, however, took a dim view of alehouses and female brewers in particular, casting them as temptresses and evildoers. As men became more prominent in the beer-making business, women were pushed aside. By the middle of the twentieth century, beer was considered a man's drink—although thanks to the popularity of craft brews during the last few decades, that image is changing.

Fairies and Nature Spirits

Many fairies are nature spirits who serve as protectors and nurturers of nature. Fairies are powerful beings who come in many forms, including the spirits who guide and guard the natural world. Some accounts say these spirits actually animate plants—they're the life force within all things in nature. So whenever you work with nature, when you do spells with herbs or other botanicals, you're working with the fairies too.

Tree Fairies According to Greek mythology, every tree had its own fairy in residence, known as a dryad. When the tree died, the fairy departed.

Nature fairies usually steer clear of humans—they don't much like people, and who can blame them considering what we've done to planet Earth? But they'll work with witches and other ecologically minded people whose goal is to benefit all beings. If you're a green witch, you probably already have the fairies' seal of approval. Kitchen witches and others who do herbal healing would be wise to connect with these spirits and earn their favor.

How can you please the nature fairies? Plant a garden if you have room; otherwise, grow a few fresh herbs in containers in a window box or in your kitchen. Nix all chemical fertilizers and pesticides. Buy organic produce. Support local farmers and gardeners who practice earth-honoring ways. Donate to organizations that protect the environment.

Interest in fairy magic appears to be growing among witches today—indeed, associations between fairies and witches have existed for centuries (see my book *The Modern Witchcraft Guide to Fairies* for more information). Invite the fae to bring their knowledge and powers to the plants you use for food, healing, and magic work—they can strengthen and improve the plants' potency.

Use caution when working with fairies, though. They're not sweet, benign creatures who have your best interests at heart. Most legends describe them as immoral tricksters who play pranks on humans—they can even be downright dangerous. And don't, repeat don't, eat or drink with the fae, or you'll risk slipping into their magical realm forever. Remember Washington Irving's story "Rip Van Winkle"? In it, Rip shares liquor with fairies in the Catskill Mountains and falls asleep for twenty years.

It's okay to leave food for them, however. In fact, doing so can help you get on their good side. Folklore tells us fairies like milk, honey, and sweets (homemade, not the prepackaged stuff laden with preservatives and chemicals). Some accounts say they're fond of wine and beer too!

Part 2

Building Your Craft As a Kitchen Witch

The everyday is magic for the kitchen witch. Kitchen witches develop, practice, and ply their trade at home, and because of this, they often have some unique practices. Due to the fact that they use elements of their homes in their magic—even utilizing common kitchen items as magical tools—kitchen witches may not have a separate toolbox of magical instruments as other practitioners of the craft do. There are no uniforms, no special texts, no unique prayers, and no obligatory tools. The kitchen witch's tools are likely to be practical and utilitarian rather than ornate and decorative—but this in no way diminishes the power or presence of them.

In the chapters that follow, you'll learn more about a kitchen witch's tools of the trade and how to use them both in cooking your meals and performing your magic. You'll also learn about choosing ingredients that support your intentions as well as how to set up your kitchen so that it's comfortable for you and enables you to generate the outcomes you desire.

In addition, you'll learn about ways to take your magic beyond your own kitchen—including how to connect to other witches and ways to work your magic in your own community, as well as ways to get the whole family involved. Finally, you'll learn about the eight sabbats, or holy days, that witches celebrate and how to incorporate your kitchen witch sensibilities to open your home, build new traditions with your family and friends, and witness the turning of the seasons through festivals, celebrations, and rituals that tie together ancient witchcraft to modern holidays.

Chapter 3

Getting Started with Kitchen Witchery

WITCHCRAFT COMES IN MANY FLAVORS, each with its own ideas, practices, guidelines, rites—even its own pantheon of deities. In kitchen witchery, you'll find some areas are similar to or compatible with other traditions. For example, many of the tools magic workers of other stripes use in their workings have counterparts in kitchen witchcraft. This chapter will look at the principal tools of the craft, their traditional meanings and purposes, and the crossover between these well-known ceremonial objects and the mundane implements kitchen witches employ in everyday magic. You'll see how these tools have connections with the feminine and masculine forces in the universe and with the four elements: fire, earth, air, and water. You'll also learn how to cleanse, consecrate, charge, and care for your magic tools so they serve you long and well in your kitchen and elsewhere in your life.

Tools and Their Energies

If you've been walking the path of the witch for a while, you're already familiar with many of the tools used. You probably own some and use them in your spells and rituals. But if you're new to the witchy life, this chapter will introduce you to items you may want to incorporate into your magical workings.

Each of these tools has symbolic as well as practical purposes. Its shape, the material it's made of, the colors you use to decorate it all hold meanings that you can draw upon in your magic work. The pentagram, a tool frequently associated with witchcraft, is a good example. The five points of the star symbolize the five "points" of the human body: the head, arms, and legs. Its symbolism suggests one of its most popular uses: physical protection.

Leonardo's Pentagram You've probably seen pictures of the pen-and-ink drawing Italian artist Leonardo da Vinci did circa 1490 called *Vitruvian Man*. Although the Renaissance master intended it as a diagram showing the ideal human proportions, if you look at it from a witch's perspective, you'll notice it also depicts a pentagram.

Kitchen witches will instantly spot similarities between the primary tools magic workers of many genres have employed since antiquity and the everyday items with which they prepare food. In kitchen witchery, the mundane and the magical are entwined. After all, food is a basic need, essential for our earthly existence. What could be more magical than nurturing life?

Remember, though, the tools themselves don't create the magic. You do. Magic is all in your mind. However, bringing ritual tools into your spellwork helps you focus your mind so you bring more power and clarity to your practice.

FEMININE AND MASCULINE ENERGIES

The universe is made up of feminine and masculine forces, yin and yang, goddess and god. These polarities combine to produce wholeness. Both are necessary to create life. You see these forces depicted in a magic worker's four major ritual tools—the wand, chalice, pentagram, and athame or ritual dagger—and in colors, shapes, materials, numbers—just about everything. The food you eat contains feminine and/or masculine energies too (more about this in Part 3). Don't think "woman" or "man" here, though; we're talking about energies, not genders.

In the world of magic, the feminine or yin force is receptive; the masculine or yang force is active. Masculine tools stimulate, direct, and project energy; feminine tools hold, nurture, and give form to energy. The wand, athame (ritual dagger), and sword are obviously phallic in shape; consequently, they're considered masculine. The shapes of the chalice, cauldron, and bell represent the womb and feminine energy.

THE FOUR ELEMENTS IN MAGIC

The four elements—fire, earth, air, and water—are the building blocks of our world. You see them manifested physically all around you, but witches work with the symbolism of the elements as well. Each has its own unique properties and purposes in spellcraft.

The fire element's most obvious manifestation is actual fire. You call upon this element to generate movement, for inspiration and enthusiasm, for courage and confidence, and to speed up a spell's action. The wand is a fire tool in magic. So are candles. Astrologers know Aries, Leo, and

Sagittarius as the fire signs of the zodiac. In kitchen witchery, the stove is the primary fire tool, although some people work their magic on barbecue grills, over firepits, or in fireplaces. Dining by candlelight also taps the energy of the fire element.

You see the element of earth in the ground on which you stand, the soil and stones that provide your foundation. In spellwork, you tap this element when you seek stability, permanence, security, patience, and endurance. Witches consider the pentagram an earth tool. So are crystals and other stones. In astrology, the earth signs are Taurus, Virgo, and Capricorn. A kitchen witch may wear a pentagram or display one in her home for protection. Consider imprinting the symbol on a piecrust, a loaf of bread, or a batch of cookies. When you use salt in cooking, you're also working with the earth element.

The element of air is all around you, in the wind and in the air you breathe. You engage the element symbolically in your thinking, when you communicate with others, and when you share ideas verbally or in written form. Thus, air plays a role in most spells. Affirmations, incantations, chants, sigils, and words of power all utilize the element of air. The ritual dagger known as an athame is considered an air tool. In kitchen witchery, knives fill this role. Gemini, Libra, and Aquarius are the air signs in astrology.

Which Way the Wind Blows Many ancient civilizations believed the wind was influenced by the direction from which it originated. This idea translates into magical methods quite nicely. For example, if a wind blows from the south, it can generate passion, warmth, or enthusiasm in spellcraft. If a wind moves from the west, it stimulates intuition and imagination.

The water element is physically evident in the oceans, rivers, lakes, and rain. It's also present in all liquids. In kitchen witchery, the beverages you drink as well as many of the meals you prepare include water. Because water is essential for life, you connect it with nurturing and nourishment. And of course, you wash in it, so water represents cleansing and purifying in spellwork as well as in ordinary life. The water element also expresses itself in your emotions. In astrology, the water signs are Cancer, Scorpio, and Pisces. The chalice is a water tool, used to hold magic potions and liquids in rituals and spells. For kitchen witches, drinking glasses can serve as chalices in everyday rituals.

Kitchen Witchery Tools

Let's take a closer look at the tools you may want to use in traditional spellcraft and in kitchen witchery. If you're a seasoned witch, you're already familiar with these. If you're a beginner, these brief guidelines will help you decide which tools to include in your own magical toolbox. You might want to start with a few, then add more as you go along—don't feel like you have to rush out and buy every item you see in your favorite New Age store or online magic shop. Kitchen witches do not need all the latest gadgets to prepare great meals and perform effective spells.

THE WAND

The idea of using a magic wand to turn your boss into a toad or to make your rival vanish may be tempting, but that's not how it works. A wand's main purpose is to direct energy. If you want to send energy to a person, place, or thing, just aim your magic wand in that direction and then mentally project the energy on its way. You can also attract energy with a wand—point it at the sky to draw down power from the heavens, or at the ground to draw up the energy of Mother Earth. Magic workers often use wands to cast circles around designated spaces where spells or rituals will take place.

Traditionally, witches and other magic workers fashioned wands from wood. However, you may prefer one made of metal, glass, or another material—it's totally up to you. Let your intuition guide you in selecting this and other tools. Make sure you can wield the wand easily. It should be at least 6 inches long, but if you want something with a bit more heft and it feels comfortable in your hand, go for it.

Kitchen witches may see similarities between a wand and a wooden spoon. After all, you use a spoon to direct energy when you stir a soup or stew on your stove. Your intention is what matters—if you consider your kitchen tools magical implements, you imbue them with the power to assist you in enacting your will. You may even want to decorate certain wooden spoons with astrological, alchemical, or personal symbols that hold meaning to you.

THE PENTAGRAM

This five-pointed star surrounded by a circle should be displayed with a single point upright, two down, and two out to the sides so it represents the human body. The circle symbolizes wholeness, unity, and connection. As mentioned earlier, the pentagram is a tool of protection, and it may be fashioned of any material, depending on how you intend to use it.

Popular as jewelry, pentagrams are a favorite witchy adornment, sometimes decorated with protection gems such as bloodstone, turquoise, or amber. Some witches prefer silver pentagrams because silver is a feminine metal and the pentagram embodies feminine energy due to its connection with the earth element, but wear what feels right to you. You may want to acquire a small pentagram charm and slip it into an amulet along with a few protection herbs (see Part 3). Put one in the glove compartment of your car to ensure safe travels. You may even decide to get a pentagram tattooed on your body to provide permanent protection.

Kitchen witches may choose to display images of pentagrams in their kitchens or throughout their homes to safeguard themselves, their loved ones, and their property. Carve them on the candles you burn at dinner to provide protection as well as ambience. Pentagrams also make attractive decorations for trivets, breadboards, coasters, and serving trays.

Pentagrams and Lone Stars If you visit Texas, you'll see pentagrams everywhere—hanging in doorways, on gates, and in gardens; laid out in paving stones in town squares; and adorning belt buckles, beer steins, saddles, automobile license plates—just about every object you can possibly imagine. Most people, of course, don't realize the state's "lone star" has another meaning.

THE ATHAME

A magic worker's ritual dagger, the athame is usually a short, straight, double-edged knife, although some witches prefer a curved one that symbolizes the crescent moon. A weapon of the "spiritual warrior," it's not used to cut physical objects. Rather, it slices through psychological blockages and obstacles; severs limiting ties, behaviors, and addictions; and dispels unwanted entities. Some magic workers use it instead of a wand for circle casting. Usually, an athame is made of metal, but whether that's steel, iron, brass, silver, or gold is up to you—you may even prefer a dagger with a crystal blade.

As a rule, ritual magic tools aren't used for mundane purposes. In kitchen witchery, however, that rule may not be valid. To kitchen witches, every act holds reverence and spiritual significance. Therefore, you may choose to apply your athame to ordinary acts that traditional magicians might not consider appropriate for ritual tools. Again, the decision is up to the individual witch.

Of course, you'll immediately note the connection between an athame and a kitchen knife. What cook doesn't have a favorite knife? One of the most important and oft-used implements in any kitchen, the well-honed knife gets into the act in the preparation of virtually all meals. It's a small step from seeing a knife as a practical tool to one you can use for magical workings—especially when you, the witch, infuse it with your own power and intention.

The Blooded Blade? Tradition says an athame should never have drawn blood. But from the perspective of kitchen witchery, a knife used for the preparation of a meal that includes meat may circumvent that dictum. Using a special knife in the ritual sacred hunt, to field dress an animal taken magically and with reverence, can be a way to consecrate the tool. It also establishes a spiritual bond between the hunter, the prey, the kitchen witch who prepares the meal, and those who eat it with gratitude.

THE CHALICE

A witch's chalice may be an ornate vessel engraved with symbols and embellished with gemstones, or a simple goblet made of silver, crystal, ceramic, or another material of your choosing. As mentioned earlier, the chalice represents the element of water—no surprise, considering its main purpose is to hold libations shared in ceremonies and potions used in spells. Its long handle enables participants in a ritual to pass the chalice easily from one person to another.

The Holy Grail Chalice The most famous of all chalices, the legendary Holy Grail, is believed in Christian tradition to be the cup from which Jesus drank at the Last Supper and in which Joseph of Arimathea collected Jesus' blood after his Crucifixion. Today, this chalice is rumored to lie at the bottom of the Chalice Well in Glastonbury, England.

Japanese scientist Masaru Emoto in his bestselling book *The Hidden Messages in Water* argued that water absorbs images with which it comes into contact—words and pictures actually affect the molecules in the water. Therefore, you'll want to make certain the symbols, gemstones, and decorations on your chalice have positive associations for you. In spellwork, you can choose images to imprint water or other beverages with your intentions. One way to do this is to select a tarot card that represents your objective, such as the Two of Cups for a happy romantic relationship, and then set your water-filled chalice on the card. The picture and meaning on the card will be transferred to the water.

Usually, magical practitioners recommend using your chalice only for magical purposes, ritual brews, and special potions—not to drink a soda at lunch. Kitchen witches, however, might take a different view. You may consider the regular drinking glasses you use daily to be ritual tools and the beverages you drink from them to be sacred libations. Perhaps you'll decide to keep an ornate chalice for ceremonial purposes and designate certain wine goblets or other glasses for everyday magic.

THE CAULDRON

As with the chalice, a cauldron's shape brings to mind the womb and symbolizes feminine energy. Traditionally, a cauldron is a three-legged vessel made of cast iron, but you may prefer one made of another metal, ceramic, or any fireproof material. You can cook a meal in a cauldron or build a ritual fire in one. A kitchen witch may own a magic cauldron, but you can also view your regular cooking pots and saucepans as "cauldrons" in which you concoct sacred meals.

Brigid's Cauldron Artists often depict Brigid, the fiery Celtic goddess, stirring a cauldron that signifies her creative power. We celebrate her sabbat on Imbolc (February 1–2), also known as Brigid's Day and Candlemas. *Imbolc* means "in the belly," and in goddess-based spirituality, Brigid is considered a goddess of creativity who nurtures children of the mind as well as of the body.

CANDLES

The most common tools in a witch's toolbox, candles have all sorts of uses in spells, rituals, and everyday life. Just as soft candlelight brings a congenial ambience to a dinner table, it sets a mystical mood in a ritual. Candles symbolize the fire element and spirit, the energizing force that activates magic work.

You'll probably want to keep an assortment of candles on hand, in various sizes, shapes, and colors. Tapers make a lovely addition to any meal. Pillar candles, because they burn for hours, are good choices for spells that take a while to enact. Votives are preferable for shorter spells. Witches on the go like candles in tins or jars because they're easy to transport. Candles shaped like human beings serve as poppets in magical workings. Kitchen witches may want to stock up on birthday candles—you needn't wait for a birthday to burn candles on a cake or cupcakes.

Birthday Magic Undoubtedly, you're familiar with the custom of making a wish, then blowing out candles on your birthday cake. What you may not realize, however, is that when you do this, you're performing a simple but powerful good luck spell. Astrologers know your birthday is an important, high-octane day when celestial forces align to spotlight your unique role on this planet. It's also a time when the cosmos supports your magical endeavors.

Colors hold symbolic significance for us, so consider a candle's color when using it in a spell. Red and pink are popular colors for love spells because they represent passion and affection, respectively. Silver and gold bring to mind wealth, so choose these for money spells. Black candles signify protection, banishing, and limitations. (The next chapter will talk more about color symbolism.)

Scents, too, influence your spells and rituals. Smell is essential to your enjoyment of food, sex, and other pleasures in life. The healing modality known as aromatherapy uses the essential oils in plants for psychological and medicinal purposes: lavender to encourage relaxation, grapefruit to bring mental clarity, rose to inspire romantic feelings. You can purchase scented candles, but be sure to look for only those that contain pure, organic essential oils for magic work. Better yet, acquire an assortment of high-quality essential oils whose properties serve your purposes and dress your candles with them. Blend two or more, if you like, to fine-tune a spell. Also avoid commercial candles made from petroleum-based products and those with wicks that contain lead—beeswax and soy with cotton wicks are preferable. You may even want to make your own candles so you capture the exact qualities you seek for your workings.

Burning candles on the dining room table may seem to be only a pretty, perhaps romantic way to provide illumination at mealtime. But to a kitchen witch, this deceptively simple practice is a ritual that enhances the food you eat, the companionship you share, and the magic you bring to bear.

THE BESOM

Used to sweep away disruptive, imbalanced, or unwanted energies, a besom is a witch's broom, often made of twigs tied together to a handle and perhaps decorated with magical symbols or other images that hold meaning for the witch. For kitchen witches, this innocuous-looking tool may have practical as well as symbolic uses. An ordinary broom intended for sweeping your kitchen floor or cleaning up ashes from the fireplace may double as a magic besom. Choose one made of a natural material such as broomcorn, straw, rattan, yucca, or bamboo instead of synthetic fibers. You might even enjoy fashioning your own besom.

CRYSTALS

Most witches are fond of quartz crystals and use them in myriad ways in their practice. One of crystals' many properties is the ability to retain information, which is why they are used in computers. Crystals hold energy, images, thoughts, emotions—pretty much anything with which they come into contact. You can "program" a crystal for a specific purpose—for example, to provide protection—by telling it what you want it to do or by holding the crystal to your third eye and visualizing your intention. You can also set a crystal on a picture, such as a tarot card, to imprint the crystal with that imagery.

The Power of Quartz Quartz crystals amplify the energy of whatever they touch. Add them to talismans and amulets to boost the power of the other ingredients and to strengthen the magic.

Pointed crystals can be used to send energy. For this reason, some witches like to affix a crystal point at the end of a magic wand. Aim the point in the direction you've chosen and envision energy shooting out from the crystal toward the person, place, or thing that is the object of your intention. You can also draw in energy with the crystal. Instead of imagining energy flowing out from the crystal toward your objective, visualize the crystal sucking up energy from a source (such as the moon) and holding it until you're ready to use it.

There are so many ways to use crystals, but here are some popular ones:

- Wear or carry them for protection.
- Put them in the glove compartment of your car to ensure safe journeys.
- Dowse with one hung on a short chain.
- Scry with one—crystal balls are best for this purpose.
- Charge a magic potion with a crystal.
- Sleep with one under your pillow to bring prophetic dreams.
- Place an abundance crystal in the cash drawer of your business to increase sales.
- Put one or more on your altar to attract positive energy and enhance your rituals.

Unlike the other tools already discussed, crystals are living entities with consciousness and should be treated with the utmost respect. Don't drill holes in them. Don't let your kids play with them. When you aren't using them, store or display them in a safe place. Over time, you'll develop special relationships with your crystals, just as you would with good friends.

> **Individual Properties of Crystals** Some crystals possess special qualities a kitchen witch will find valuable. Citrine's cleansing properties, for instance, make it ideal for clearing unwanted energies from other tools. Rose quartz's gentle, loving vibrations inspire congeniality at a dinner with family or friends. Crystals that have other smaller crystals growing inside them, known as abundance crystals, attract abundance of all kinds.

Cleansing, Consecrating, and Charging Your Tools

What gives a wand, athame, or other witch's tool its magic? You do. Your willpower, your imagination, your energy, and your intention transform an ordinary stick of wood or a stainless steel blade into an object of awesome power.

CLEANSING YOUR TOOLS

Before you use a tool in magic work, you'll want to get rid of dust, dirt, and energetic vibrations that accumulated on the tool before you obtained it. This is especially important if you've chosen to use antique objects that other witches have employed in the past—you don't want their stuff interfering with your workings. From a practical standpoint, as a kitchen witch, you need to wash whatever implements you cook with to avoid contamination.

Usually, this process is simple enough. Just wash the tool with mild soap and water while you envision its being cleared of all harmful, disruptive, and imbalanced energies. You might want to cleanse the tool by holding it in the smoke of burning sage or incense for a minute or so to further purify it. Wiping it with essential oils known for their cleansing effects can be beneficial too. Oils of tea tree, basil, rosemary, and lemon are good choices—just make sure whatever you use is nontoxic and won't damage the material of the tool.

CONSECRATING YOUR TOOLS

The ritual of consecrating your magical tools can be as simple or elaborate as you want it to be. Here you dedicate your tools to a particular purpose—to work with you to enact your will, for example—and transform them from ordinary objects into magical ones. In so doing, you create a sacred bond with your tools that will last for as long as you choose, perhaps forever. This is *your* tool, and it answers to no one else but you. Nor should anyone else use it.

You may speak directly to your wand, athame, and so on, giving them direction as you would an honored assistant and explaining how you will work together. If you like, you can choreograph special movements, mudras, steps, or other actions that have meaning for you.

Some witches invite deities to participate in the consecration ritual as well as in the work they perform with their magic tools. Although you can find prepared scripts for doing this, try designing your own ritual, one that expresses your individual beliefs and intentions. The more you personalize it, the more powerful the experience will be.

CHARGING YOUR TOOLS

Finally, you'll need to "charge" your tools to activate them. This step formally kicks them into gear and sets them on their path to serving you in spellcraft. Admittedly, these are inanimate objects, but you're working magic with and through them to accomplish your objectives. Charging gives your tools a resonance you can feel when you use them, as if they were, indeed, living things. Think of a singing bowl through which sounds vibrate when you strike it with a mallet. Enlivening your magic tools is a bit like that.

You may want to use sunlight to charge a wand, water to charge a chalice. Playing music is a good way to charge a tool. Drumming or striking a gong can be effective too. Again, try designing your own charging ritual and infusing it with as much energy, emotion, and power as you can.

Four Elements Charging Technique This easy and popular technique brings together the four elements: fire, earth, air, and water. Mix salt and water in a bowl to combine the elements of earth and water. Light incense to unite the elements of fire and air. Sprinkle the tool with salt water as you say aloud, "With earth and water I charge you to do my will." Then hold the tool in the smoke from the incense for a few moments while you say, "With fire and air I charge you to do my will." After completing your ritual, dry off your tools—salt water will corrode metal—then store them in a safe place until you're ready to use them in your magical workings.

Handling and Storing Tools and Ingredients

It's generally believed that no one except the witch, wizard, or other spell caster who has consecrated a magic tool should use that tool or even handle it. This precept can get a bit sticky for kitchen witches, however, whose tools may include everyday objects such as knives, drinking glasses, and cooking pots.

You may choose to designate certain implements as your "special" tools and insist that members of your household abide by a hands-off policy where these are concerned. You can repeat the process of cleansing, consecrating, and charging magical tools whenever someone else touches them, although this can get rather time-consuming. You might create a modified version of the cleansing ritual, perhaps visualizing your tools purified by white light after each use. Or you can take a more relaxed view, realizing that your kitchen utensils and appliances are physical objects that enable you to do your work. What matters most are your intentions and the energy you invest in your craft. The tools that make this possible are means to an end.

How witches choose to store their tools will differ from person to person. If you're a kitchen witch who keeps an array of ceremonial tools in addition to everyday items that have practical purposes, you'll probably want to store them in separate places for convenience and to avoid mix-ups. If your living space is large enough, you might designate an area of your home separate from your kitchen for ceremonial workings.

Herbs and spices, food items, and perishables require careful storage to avoid deterioration. Part 3 of this book is an encyclopedia of magical edibles that discusses many herbs and spices that have both culinary and magical uses. As a cook and a witch, you'll have your favorites, things you go to on a regular basis. For convenience, you may keep the oft-used ones in a handy spice rack and stash the special occasion items in an unobtrusive, cool, dark spot. Remember that dried herbs and spices have shelf lives—some last quite a while, others not so much. As they age, they lose both their flavor and their potency for spellwork. As a general rule, toss anything that's more than a year old.

If possible, grow your own fresh herbs in containers, a kitchen window box, or a garden. Fresh greens provide more flavor and more magical power—and they make a pretty addition to your kitchen. In spells, fresh ingredients act more quickly and have a livelier energy. Dried ones have less zing but give longer-lasting results.

Chapter 4

A Place for Working Magic

EARLY KITCHENS WERE SIMPLY INDOOR hearth fires, not individual rooms as they are today. Over time, they evolved into multipurpose work spaces where a variety of activities took place. Cooking, naturally, was a main function of the kitchen, but people in the past also did laundry and bathed there. They made candles; preserved food; concocted medicines; sewed, spun, and wove cloth; and performed many other tasks. Because the kitchen was the warmest room in the house, children learned their lessons there, and adults read by the fire's light.

Modern kitchen witches are reviving the practices of their forebears. Many prepare herbal remedies in their kitchens; some grow herbs and other plants in containers or window boxes. You might can food or craft candles, soap, and personal-care products in your kitchen. Maybe you've carved out space for a computer, or your kids do their homework at the kitchen table. Of course, you also perform spells here. And you most likely still congregate with loved ones in the kitchen to share conversation and friendship, as well as food.

This chapter will discuss how to prepare your kitchen to become a place for you to perform your magic. Before you begin, though, take time to think about how you'll perform the dual duties of your craft in this space. You may want to check out online sites, peruse magazines, and talk with other witches to get ideas. Once you have some ideas, you'll be ready to declutter, clean, and create the perfect kitchen for your practice.

Decluttering Your Kitchen

Each kitchen is a unique expression of the people who use it. Because this is the kitchen witch's temple, apothecary, and place for doing magic as well as where you prepare meals, it's important that the space be designed with all these functions in mind. If you're building a home or renovating one, you have the luxury of creating a kitchen from scratch, exactly to your specifications. But most people will have to work with what they've got. Nevertheless, you can tailor your kitchen to your needs with some careful planning and a little esoteric knowledge.

GETTING RID OF CLUTTER

How often have you become frustrated because you couldn't find the tool or spice or container you needed? Are your kitchen cabinets jammed with things you rarely use? Do you have many more twist ties, rubber bands, or plastic bags than you'll ever need? Does your refrigerator harbor leftovers you've forgotten about and that have turned to mold? If so, it's probably time to do some decluttering.

Most of us have more "stuff" than we need or use. From a practical perspective, all that stuff can interfere with the efficient operation of your kitchen—in some cases, clutter may even present a hazard. Symbolically, clutter has emotional and psychological connections, such as fear of loss or scarcity, holding on to the past, and resistance to change.

Clutter Correlations Clutter can represent many things:

- *Confusion:* areas in your life that are uncertain or unresolved
- *Old baggage:* outdated ideas and attitudes that you're still clinging to
- *Obstacles:* limitations or blockages that inhibit your progress

As you can imagine, clutter presents big problems for kitchen witches. Focus and clarity are essential to effective magic work, as you know. If your kitchen is a tangled mess of disorganized paraphernalia, if you can't locate the tools or ingredients you need for a spell, you might get rattled or find it hard to concentrate on your intention. And because all objects hold energy, old stuff you don't even remember you own may contribute subtle influences that interfere with your current goals.

Pick a section of your kitchen that corresponds to an area of your life where you'd like to see some improvement (see the following section about feng shui). Start by getting rid of things you never use or don't really like. Everything you decide to keep should have a purpose and positive associations. Consider donating items that are in good shape to a charity, which activates the cycle of giving and receiving. Start slow, so you don't get overwhelmed. Perhaps you'll want to enlist the help of a friend or family members.

You may notice that decluttering stirs up emotions and memories. The process will also spur changes in your life, which is a good reason to take it slow. Clear away a little, then wait and see what happens. Many people feel the energy in their kitchens seems lighter, livelier, and more joyful after they've eliminated a lot of unwanted stuff. Quite likely, you'll discover new opportunities come your way because you've made room for them.

Feng Shui in the Kitchen

The ancient art of feng shui has been a staple in China for thousands of years, but it only gained popularity in the West in the 1980s. Feng shui combines commonsense design principles with symbolism, mysticism, and magic to bring health, wealth, and happiness into your life.

Although there are many schools of thought in feng shui, its Western adherents consider your home to be a reflection of you, and they link the various sections, or "guas," of your living space with the different areas of your life. To assess which areas are functioning smoothly and which ones are out of balance, feng shui practitioners superimpose an octagon-shaped diagram known as a bagua over a floor plan of your home. This allows them to see which parts of your home correspond to health, wealth, relationships, public image, and so on, and to pinpoint problems. By making adjustments in certain places in your home, you can change your life. (You can find images of the bagua online.)

You can evaluate your kitchen in the same way, by envisioning an image of the bagua laid over it. Stand with your back to the door you use most often to enter and exit your kitchen. Looking in, the area immediately in front of you, sometimes called the career or self gua, represents your self-image, identity, aspirations, and so on. The section to your immediate right corresponds to friends, colleagues, and travel. The portion to your immediate left relates to knowledge and spirituality. The distant-left sector relates to wealth, and the far-right one signifies marriage and primary relationships. The part between the wealth and knowledge guas represents family and community, and the one between the relationships and friends guas concerns creativity and children. The area in front and farthest from you signifies your public image and the future. The central portion of the room correlates with your health.

Wind and Water *Feng shui* translates as "wind and water." Its objective is to direct and circulate life energy, or chi, through your home in such a way that it symbolizes a pleasant breeze or a gently flowing stream. This smooth, even movement of chi creates harmony in your environment.

Once you've identified which parts of your kitchen correspond to which parts of your life, you can start to see where you might want to make some changes. For example, if the wealth gua in your kitchen is dark, it may be a sign that your financial picture is dim. Adding more light in that sector can brighten your opportunities and increase your income. If you keep your knives in the relationship gua of your kitchen, it may indicate that you and your partner fight a lot. Relocate the knives, and you'll likely notice an easing of the tension between you.

Feng shui isn't difficult, and it produces results quickly. No matter what the problem is—and most kitchens have problems—there's a cure for it, often a simple, inexpensive cure. You'll find many books and other resources available, including my book *10-Minute Feng Shui*, that can take the mystery out of this amazingly effective system of magic.

Using Symbolism in Your Kitchen's Design

Symbols embody the essence of whatever they stand for—they aren't merely a convenient form of shorthand. That's why they have such power, why they appear in diverse and widely separated cultures, and why they have endured for millennia. You react to symbols subconsciously and emotionally, rather than from a place of logic or rational thinking.

Spellwork relies heavily on the use of symbols. Sympathetic magic is a good example. The basic philosophy of sympathetic magic is simple: Like attracts like. This means that an item can symbolize or serve as a representative for another item that's similar to it in some way. It also means that the similarities are not coincidental; they signify a connection—physical, spiritual, energetic, or otherwise—between the two items. Ginseng root, for example, resembles the human body, a similarity that some healers believe contributes to ginseng's medicinal properties. Let's look at how you can incorporate some common symbols into your kitchen.

COLOR SYMBOLISM

In the practice of magic, colors correspond to the four elements: fire, earth, air, and water. Red is associated with the fire element, green with earth, yellow with air, and blue with water.

The fire element is linked with action, vitality, enthusiasm, passion, inspiration, and courage. So, if you want to speed up or spice up an area in your life, use the color red in the part of your kitchen that corresponds to that part of your life. Let's say you'd like your love life to be more exciting. You could put a vase of red roses in the marriage/relationship gua. Every time you look at the roses, you'll be reminded of your intention.

Witches connect the element of earth with stability, permanence, security, and endurance. If an area of your life feels chaotic or unsteady, put some green in the section of your kitchen that relates to that area. Does money seem to flow out as soon as it comes in? Place one or more healthy plants in green ceramic pots in the wealth gua to stabilize your financial situation.

Yellow is the color of the air element. Magic workers associate air with communication, mental activity, and intellectual pursuits. Want to improve communication with your kids? Consider painting the wall or cabinets in the children gua yellow.

We connect blue with the element of water. Water represents emotions, intuition, and purification. If you're experiencing a lot of stress or emotional upset related to your job, add some blue to the career gua of your kitchen to calm things down.

Cultural Correspondences Colors have different connections and symbolism in different cultures. For instance, Chinese brides wear red, a color of good fortune in that culture. In China, white is considered a color of mourning. For witches, black denotes power, not grief. Kitchen witches in the US can use green in prosperity spells because their paper money is green, but that might not work for witches in other countries.

Here's a list of colors and their associations:

- **Red:** vitality, passion, anger, heat, daring
- **Orange:** confidence, creativity, warmth, enthusiasm, generosity, joy
- **Yellow:** happiness, creativity, optimism, ideas, communication
- **Green:** growth, health, fertility, wealth
- **Light blue:** peace, clarity, hope, kindness
- **Royal blue:** independence, insight, imagination, truth
- **Indigo:** intuition, serenity, mental power
- **Purple:** wisdom, spiritual power, connection with higher realms
- **Pink:** love, friendship, affection, sociability
- **White:** purity, clarity, protection
- **Black:** wisdom, permanence, mystery, banishing, limitations
- **Brown:** stability, practicality, grounding in the physical world

Colors also have personal symbolism. We all have favorite colors and colors we don't like much. For most people, yellow brings to mind sunshine and happiness, but maybe it represents cowardice to you. The colors you decide to include in your kitchen should hold positive associations for you.

Symbolic Shapes

Shapes, too, have symbolic associations, and you react to them often without realizing it. For witches, the circle is one of the most familiar and powerful shapes. You cast circles around the places where you perform spells and enact rituals. The circle forms an energetic barrier that keeps unwanted energies out of your sacred space so they can't disrupt or interfere with what you're doing. The circle also holds the energy you raise and the magic you do until you're ready to release them.

The following list gives some of the common shape associations in magic work:

- **Circle:** wholeness, unity, completion, protection
- **Square or rectangle:** stability, structure, permanence
- **Triangle and arrow:** movement, pointing in a direction; upward-pointing triangle symbolizes masculine energy, downward-pointing represents feminine energy
- **Five-pointed star:** hope, protection, the human body
- **Six-pointed star:** merger of masculine and feminine energies
- **Straight line:** defining boundaries, connection or separation
- **Horizontal line:** rest, stability, feminine energy, the earth plane
- **Vertical line:** ambition, instability, masculine energy, the sky
- **Wavy or curved line:** graceful, fluid movement

Symbols of Creativity The cross is one of Christianity's most important symbols, and the Star of David is one of Judaism's. But behind the familiar meanings of these images lies another interpretation that transcends specific religious beliefs. The vertical line and the upward-pointing triangle represent the masculine or yang force in the universe. The horizontal line and the downward-pointing triangle signify the feminine or yin force. When these symbols intersect, they express the union of the two forces that is necessary for creation.

Look around your kitchen and pay attention to the shapes of things you use there. Think about how you can incorporate the symbolism of these objects into your magical practice. Cabinets, countertops, and most appliances are either square or rectangular. So are trays, baking pans, cookie sheets, and casserole dishes. If your objective is to create stability or structure, cook and serve meals in these utensils.

Plates, bowls, cups, glasses, pots, and skillets are usually round. Cooking, eating, and drinking from these can promote harmony, unity, and wholeness. Maybe your kitchen or dining table is round. Round tables encourage congeniality because everyone seated at the table can see and talk with everyone else easily. Round tables also eliminate the sense of hierarchy that rectangular tables engender—there's no head or foot, so diners feel more equal.

Straight lines are depicted in silverware, although spoons also feature ovals. When you set the table, lay cutlery in a direction or arrangement that corresponds to your intention.

NUMBER SYMBOLISM

Numerology—the spiritual study of numbers—is thousands of years old. Esoteric traditions have long honored and understood the symbolism of numbers. Each number has a sacred meaning as well as a mundane one, and each possesses its own special characteristics.

Numbers are among the most common and frequently used symbols. They also provide kitchen witches with a simple "device" for magic work. And because most people don't understand the hidden meanings of numbers, you can use them to cast spells without altering anyone else. If you're not already familiar with number symbolism, here's a list of the basic meanings:

- **One:** individuality, beginnings, focus
- **Two:** partnership, union, duality, balance/imbalance
- **Three:** self-expression, creativity, manifestation in the three-dimensional world
- **Four:** stability, perseverance, structure
- **Five:** change, instability, communication, movement
- **Six:** contentment; social interaction; community; creativity, especially in joint projects with other people
- **Seven:** inner growth, spirituality, retreat
- **Eight:** material gain, physical resources, career success, permanence, banishing
- **Nine:** wisdom, completion, fulfillment, transition

Let's say you're an artist and you want to break out of a dry spell and stimulate your creativity. Burn three royal blue candles on your table at suppertime to summon the muse and awaken your inner spark. This simple spell combines the self-expression of the number three with the imagination represented by royal blue and the inspiration of fire. Easy, right?

Three's a Charm For witches, three is a special number. Because we live in a three-dimensional world, we use the number three to seal a spell and bring it into manifestation. Speak an affirmation or incantation three times. Tie a charm bag closed with three knots. Combine three objects that relate to your purpose—such as crystals, candles, and botanicals—in a spell.

SIGILS

A sigil is a uniquely personal symbol you create in order to produce a specific result. The word comes from the Latin *sigillum*, meaning "sign." In a sense, a sigil is a way of communicating with yourself via secret code, because no one else can interpret the symbol. Although there are various techniques for designing sigils, the easiest one involves fashioning an image from letters.

Start by writing a word or a short affirmation that states your intention. Delete any letters that are repeated. For example, the word *success* contains three *s*'s and two *c*'s, but you only need to put one of each into your sigil. Entwine the remaining letters to form an image—this is where you get creative. You can use upper- and/or lowercase letters, block letters, or script. Position them right side up, upside down, forward, or backward. The end result depicts your objective in a graphic manner that your subconscious understands, although it won't make sense to anyone else.

Display the sigil you've designed in a place where you'll see it often. Each time you look at the sigil, you'll instantly recognize its meaning at a deep level, and that reinforces your intention. You can also incorporate sigils into your cooking. Squirt a sigil in spicy mustard on a hot dog to increase the heat in a romantic relationship. With a fork, poke a sigil for prosperity into the crust of a loaf of whole-wheat bread. As you and your loved ones consume the sigil, you'll incorporate its meaning and your good wishes into every fiber of your being.

LET THERE BE LIGHT

Think for a moment about how you feel when you enter a dark, shadowy place. Uncomfortable, probably. As soon as you turn on a light, you feel more at ease and confident. Light lets you see where you're going and what you're doing, but in addition to its practical purpose, light holds many symbolic connotations. We associate light with understanding, clarity, hope, happiness, truth, goodness, even life itself. Religious and spiritual traditions often connect the Divine with light and depict holy beings with glowing auras or halos.

For kitchen witches, light has a magical significance too. Light focuses energy into your space and adds power to your workings. Light also represents the sacred flame and spirit, as well as your own inner light. In ancient Rome, Vesta, the goddess of the hearth, was known as an aspect of the sacred flame. Vestal virgins kept fires burning in her honor at all times.

Pay attention to where you position lighting in your kitchen and what it shines on. Where light goes, energy flows. You may want to install various types of lighting: overhead for general illumination, spots or track lighting to highlight certain areas, dimmers that let you adjust the amount of light, and so on. Candlelight may figure into your workings too.

Cleansing, Clearing, and Consecrating Your Kitchen

This section will discuss cleansing, clearing, and consecrating your entire kitchen. The cleansing part includes the obvious: wiping down counters, mopping the floor, scrubbing the sink, and cleaning the stove. But you're not only getting rid of dirt and germs, you're also removing unwanted energies that could interfere with your spellwork. Once again, your intention is paramount. As you clean, envision yourself washing away self-limiting attitudes, old habits that no longer serve you, grudges, animosities, regrets, anxieties, and other ideas and emotions that could negatively impact your magic. You might want to repeat an affirmation or incantation while you work.

The next step is to clear all disruptive, imbalanced, and harmful influences from your kitchen. One way to do this is to burn sage, a plant known for its purifying properties, and waft the smoke throughout the space. Or you could mist your kitchen with a clearing tonic. Fill a spray bottle with spring water, then add a few drops of refreshing essential oils such as lemon, grapefruit, mint, or tea tree. Shake the bottle three times to blend and charge the mixture, then spritz the room. When you've finished, balance the energy in your kitchen by playing a singing bowl, bells, or peaceful music.

Finally, consecrate your kitchen to your craft. Doing so transforms it from just a room in your home to your temple. This may be as simple as saying a prayer or blessing. Or you may decide to enact an elaborate ritual that expresses your purposes. If you wish, invite family members, housemates, friends, and others who'll use this sacred space to join you.

PROTECTION IN YOUR KITCHEN

Accidents can happen anywhere in your home, but the kitchen poses more risks than other places. Therefore, it's a good idea to install some protection in your kitchen. In addition to practical measures, such as keeping a fire extinguisher on hand and storing knives where children can't reach them, use magic to safeguard your kitchen. Here are some suggestions:

- Sprinkle a little sea salt in each corner of the room to protect and purify your kitchen and to banish unwanted entities from your sacred space.
- Hang a rowan or ash branch above the entrance to your kitchen. In Celtic mythology, the rowan was one of the most sacred trees, prized for its protective properties. Old Norse legends say the first woman was made from a rowan tree, the first man from an ash.
- Position a pentagram in a prominent place in your kitchen, perhaps above the stove. Witches consider the pentagram a tool of protection and a symbol of the human body.
- Grow a basil plant in a container in your kitchen. A favorite protection herb, basil is easy to grow, plus you can snip the tasty leaves to use for cooking.
- Create a protection sigil and display it where you'll see it often. Follow the directions given earlier in this chapter to design an image that's both effective and attractive.
- Paint the Norse rune *algiz* on a white stone and use it as a doorstop. Or set the stone near the entrance to your kitchen to provide protection.
- Hang an effigy of a Germanic kitchen witch, Chinese kitchen god, or other protector deity in your kitchen to guard against accidents and mishaps.

Say a Blessing Each day when you enter your kitchen, say a simple blessing for well-being, such as this traditional Irish prayer:

*May our troubles be less
And our blessings be more.
And nothing but happiness
Come through our door.*

Kitchen Altars

Many witches have altars in their homes, where they perform spells, enact rituals, meditate, commune with deities, and store their magic equipment. An altar provides a focal point for your workings, whether you work alone or with other people. In your kitchen, an altar also reminds you that the everyday activities you engage in here aren't just necessary functions; they're sacred acts.

How much space you have and how you use your kitchen will likely dictate what kind of altar you install. If you're fortunate enough to have plenty of room, you may designate a portion of your kitchen for an altar and sanctuary. Often a kitchen table or sideboard doubles as an altar. Kitchen witches who have gardens, porches, decks, patios, and barbecue grills may choose to set up outdoor altars. If space is really tight, a windowsill, a shelf, or even a hanging basket can serve as your altar. Your intention is what counts, not how big or beautiful your altar is.

WHAT SHOULD YOU PUT ON YOUR ALTAR?

What you decide to display on your kitchen altar depends on your purposes, how you practice your craft, who uses the kitchen and altar, space constraints, and many other personal circumstances. If you also have a main altar elsewhere in your home, you may opt to store your primary magic tools—wand, pentagram, athame, chalice, and so on—there, along with other items you use in your practice, such as incense, candles, and crystals, and keep your kitchen altar simple. If your only altar is in your kitchen—and especially if you don't engage in magical practices outside those of traditional kitchen witchcraft—you may choose to display only a few cherished items on your altar.

Some witches believe you should lay out all four major tools on your altar. Others recommend stashing these tools away except during rituals, spell casting, or celebrations. If you aren't comfortable coming out with your witchy beliefs, you might prefer to create a minimalistic altar that holds only a few items that, to the untrained eye, seem completely innocuous: candles, dried or fresh flowers, a favorite stone, a feather, maybe a pretty altar cloth printed with a pattern of stars. It's up to you.

Temporary Altars If space is at a premium or you have other reasons for not wanting to erect a permanent altar in your kitchen, you can create a temporary one. This might be a pretty box in which you keep a few items to use in spellwork, such as a travel candle in a tin, a few sticks of incense, a quartz crystal or two, a small pentagram, and anything else that aids your practice. Bring it out when it's time to do some magic, and store it in a safe place when you've finished.

You may choose to place things on your kitchen altar that correspond to what's in the forefront of your life at a particular time. Are you dealing with relationship problems? Focusing on your career? Planning a trip? Engaged in a financial or legal matter? Putting pertinent concerns on your altar symbolically gives them a place of honor and supports whatever magic you may be doing.

Some witches like to decorate their altars to correspond to the seasons, sabbats, or lunar cycles or to personal holidays. This keeps things fresh and current while also helping align you with the energies operating at a given time. Displaying seasonal flowers, herbs, and fruit is a pretty way to bring you into harmony with nature's cycles. You may want to mark the sabbats by setting items on your altar that relate to these holidays: candles on Imbolc, painted eggs on Ostara, a sheaf of dried grain at Mabon.

Many witches feel a special affection for certain deities. If this applies to your practice, you might like to put a figurine or other image of a beloved goddess or god on your altar. Quan Yin, a Buddhist deity associated with mercy and compassion, occupies a place of honor on both my indoor and outdoor altars. Your kitchen altar is also an ideal place to make offerings to deities.

Crystals are popular items on altars, as you might guess. Position one or more of your favorite crystals on your altar to attract positive energies and repel unwanted ones—you can program them to support your intentions. You may also want to add gemstones whose characteristics relate to your purposes: rose quartz for love, amethyst for peace, tiger's eye for prosperity, jade for good fortune, and so on. To encourage balance in your kitchen, consider displaying stones that correspond to the four elements: carnelian for fire, aventurine for earth, blue lace agate for air, aquamarine for water.

Whatever you decide to put on your altar should have positive associations for you. Otherwise, there's no "right" or "wrong" way to set up yours. An altar is as individual as the witch who creates it. It expresses what you cherish, honor, hope for, and share with the world. It's where you work, dream, pray, and give thanks. It's where you come to lay down your burdens and receive grace.

Chapter 5

Inviting Others Into Your Practice

KITCHEN WITCHERY IS RARELY A solo venture. At the heart of this branch of witchcraft is the special element kitchen witches provide for other people, namely a sense of connectivity. In this chapter, you will learn about bringing other people into your practice, witches and nonwitches alike. This chapter will take a look at fun and easy ways to get your kids and other family members involved, as well as ways to connect to folks in your community. You'll learn how community outreach can be a magical act. This chapter also covers the fundamentals of working with pets and wildlife in your practices and the basics of connecting with familiars. Finally, you'll learn about growing your own food and herbs for spellcrafting.

Getting the Whole Family Involved

Whether you are a solitary witch or a member of a coven, there is always a movement that needs your help, passion, and good energy. Inviting family members to partake in these community actions is a great way to instill these lessons into multiple generations and inspire a magical reality in the home and community at large. Witches who want to create compelling magical change in their communities and connect with like-minded people can come together to hold community-oriented actions addressing the needs of their less fortunate neighbors. You can start by meeting the people in your neighborhood who are already working on these issues.

A clothing drive at the start of fall when the weather begins to turn cold is a powerful way to assist people while honoring the changing of the seasons—and it is something the whole family can participate in. Let children pick out a piece of clothing that feels powerful or protective to them so they can pass on that energy to a child who needs this magic. Parents can go through their kids' clothes and look for items they have outgrown or never wore. Think of the clothes in your closet or dresser that you never wear like energy you are storing up and not using. Moving that energy out into your community benefits everyone involved. And just as one would energetically cleanse a tool before passing it on, make sure the clothing items you pass along are clean and in good shape as well.

Donating with Magical Intent When donating food, consider the magical qualities of the foods as well as the conditions of those who are in need. For example, spicy foods are great for protection, foods that contain cinnamon are useful for drawing in money and reversing fortune, and leafy greens can be utilized to promote health.

Connecting with food distribution collectives in your area is a way to evoke the abundance of the Goddess throughout the year and join with other magical folks who are doing this work. Start in your own pantry and look for food items you have in abundance. Many neighborhoods have started to sponsor "community fridges." These are stand-alone refrigerators and pantries, often connected to local businesses willing to supply the electricity for the refrigerators, where community members can leave donations of food, drinks, and toiletries. Folks in need can come by any time to see what has been donated and pick up what they want. You can take this one step further and reach out to restaurants and coffee shops in your area to schedule donation pickups as a way of keeping your community refrigerator topped up with tasty and magical offerings. This is also a magical opportunity to get the whole family out of the house; take everyone for a walk down to the local community fridge to stock the shelves and say a blessing over the items.

WITCHCRAFTING WITH KIDS

Getting the kids involved in your kitchen witchery may seem daunting, but it can be as simple as baking some cookies. Whip up a batch of sugar cookie dough, or make it really easy on yourself and grab a premade roll from the grocery store. With a little imagination, your basic cookie cutters can be transformed into powerful symbols. For example, a plain circle cookie cutter can create a moon, a sun, or even a pentagram. A gingerbread person cookie cutter can be used to create gods and goddesses. A candy cane can become a wand. Triangles can be turned into pyramids or symbols for the elements. Encourage children to do some research on the shapes and symbols they create and to explore the concepts they are baking. Mix up frosting in a multitude of colors and take advantage of the opportunity to discuss the magical meanings of each color. Decorate your cookies with witchy sigils or extra mystical details. Silver sprinkles on moon cookies or gold sprinkles on sun cookies will amplify the planetary vibrations and make great treats to bring to your next esbat or sabbat get-together.

SALT DOUGH ORNAMENTS

Salt dough ornaments are an excellent way to call forth the muse and create wonderful holiday keepsake treasures with the family. Salt dough is incredibly simple to make, and you can mold it into just about anything. Mix up a bowl full of dough, and as you do, take a few deep breaths and push your intentions into the dough, infusing it with your magic and good wishes. You can make deities, animals, or even actual magical sigils from the dough.

Salt Dough Recipe Here is an easy recipe to make salt dough:

- 1 cup salt
- 2 cups flour
- 1 cup warm water

In a medium bowl, mix together the salt and flour, then add the water, pouring slowly as you may need less than the 1 cup. Knead the mixture into a dough. If your dough is tough, add more water. If it is too sticky, add more flour. Now you are ready to either roll out your dough for your cookie cutters, or freehand mold your dough into shapes.

Once you have your salt dough in the shape you want, you can press beads or charms into it as well. If you want to hang your ornaments, make sure you leave a space at the top and poke a hole through the dough with a straw or pencil. Bake your ornaments at 200°F until they are hard (around 20–30 minutes). Once they are cool, use glitter and paint to bring out the details, and follow that with a coat of clear varnish (paint the front and back) to seal them. After they've dried, thread them with ribbon and they'll be ready to hang! Treated with care, salt dough ornaments can last for decades or even longer.

Working with Wildlife

Working with birds, insects, and other wildlife can be an important part of your kitchen witchery. Many witches see these creatures as an extension of Mother Nature herself. Cultivating relationships with the fauna in your world is a time-honored practice for witches. Of course, plenty of kitchen witches have pets, but fostering relationships with the wildlife in your area is equally important. Whether it is for companionship, protection, or asking for magical messages from the universe, developing and maintaining a connection with the creatures in your life can be a special type of magic all on its own.

BEES AND OTHER INSECTS

The insect world is important in the eyes of witches, who know how helpful these tiny creatures can be. Spiders are always welcome in the home of a witch. Many folks think it is bad luck to kill a spider, and folk wisdom teaches if a spider is alive in your house, that is because there is something for it to eat. Kill the spider and risk an infestation of whatever the spider has been feeding on. People around the world have worshipped this insect in multiple goddess forms, like those of the Greek Arachne and the Hopi Spider Grandmother.

Scarabs and other beetles have a holy place in the grand design too. According to some ancient Egyptian myths the sun god Ra was reborn each day and was pushed across the sky by a scarab-faced god named Khepri. Together Khepri and Ra represent creation and rebirth.

In addition, monarch butterflies are thought to be the returning souls of the dead when they make their yearly migration coinciding with the Day of the Dead in Mexico.

Perhaps most sacred of all are the bees that pollinate the plants that bear our herbs, fruits, and vegetables. The world would be a hungry place without these amazing insects. Mythology tells us the story of the Greek goddess Melissa, the goddess of the bees. Her priestesses were called the "Melissae." In Greek mythology, Melissa was a nymph who was taught the magic of honey by the bees.

The Mystical and Magical Bee Bees appeared in Egyptian hieroglyphs and often indicated royalty. One of the titles bestowed on pharaohs was "he of the sedge and bee," which referred to his role as king of upper and lower Egypt (the bee being a symbol of lower Egypt). Egyptians also regarded bees as servants of the gods, delivering messages and healing gifts from the gods to humanity.

Witches who care about bees can help them in a variety of ways. Planting indigenous (local to your area) wildflowers rich in pollen and nectar will create a food source for these important pollinators. And you don't need a yard to help bees; a window box or even a few flowerpots on your porch will do. Make sure to charge your seeds before planting by focusing your intentions for support into the seeds and the soil.

Bees also work up quite a thirst foraging and collecting nectar, especially in the summer, when they can have a hard time finding water. To help, make a bee bath. Fill a shallow birdbath, bowl, or pan with clean water and arrange pebbles, crystals, or marbles along the bottom so that they break the water's surface. Bees will land on the stones and pebbles to take a long, refreshing drink, making it the perfect watering hole.

BIRDS

Birds have always played an important role in magic and witchcraft. Ancient Romans practiced augury, or interpreting the movements of birds for messages. The ancient Greeks called it ornithomancy, and they watched flight patterns and listened to the cries of birds for magical information. In addition, the owl is a symbol of the goddess of wisdom, Athena.

Thoth, the ibis-headed Egyptian god, is worshipped for his knowledge. Native Americans in the Pacific Northwest have often depicted ravens and eagles on their totem poles, and for some tribes, birds became deities, like Crow Mother or the fabled thunderbird.

Irish folklore teaches that killing a robin will bring lifelong bad luck, perhaps because the robin is thought by some to be a pagan god in disguise. The Batswana tribe of Northern Africa never cut down the Mosu tree, because it is the roosting place for many migratory birds. And in cultures all around the world, it is thought to be good luck if a bird poops on you!

Kitchen witches can work with birds by divining messages in their flight patterns. Simply find a wide open space and watch the shapes birds make as they fly overhead, journaling whatever you see. Another form of bird divination is finding feathers. Take a moment to focus on a question. Then, go for a walk. Document any feathers you see, and look up the bird and its meaning when you get home.

Wildlife and Magical Offerings Offerings left out for wildlife should be given with no expectations. Make sure anything you provide for the wild animals, birds, and insects in your world is appropriate for them. Don't offer food or drinks covered in ashes, candle wax, or other potentially toxic elements. If you wouldn't eat it, neither should they.

Kitchen witches can call in bird magic by making their yards homes for the birds in their neighborhood. Placing feeders full of seeds and dried fruits outside during winter or offering up a shallow basin for a birdbath during summer helps local wildlife make it through the harshest months. A great way to attract birds to your yard is to plant native trees, bushes, and flowers. And when mulching fallen leaves and yard waste in fall, leave them on the ground! The decomposing plant material will become home to thousands of insects that birds will feed on.

Witches and Their Pets

For most people, pets are family members. Including them in your rituals and celebrations is easy as long as you follow a few guidelines for everyone's safety and have respect for your pets and their tolerance for unfamiliar activities.

Keep animals away from open flames like candles, torches, and bonfires. Remember, animals are generally more sensitive than humans, which is part of their special abilities. But it also means loud noises like horns, drums, and shouting can be frightening to them. If you want your pets to attend rituals, start them off slow and watch them for signs of discomfort, removing them to a quiet, calm space at the first sign of distress. Many animals' sense of smell is also much keener than yours. It is generally good practice to keep strong smells like incense and essential oils away from animals, and they should never come into contact with essential oils except under the direction of a veterinarian.

DOG DAYS

Many people believe dogs have an ability to detect spirits, and a number of cultural traditions throughout history have shown a connection between dogs and the afterlife. Cerberus was a three-headed dog from Greek mythology who guarded the gates of Hades, the land of the dead, ensuring no one passed through the gates who was not supposed to. The Aztecs worshipped a dog-headed god named Xolotl, who guided souls to the underworld. And ancient Egyptians also worshipped a dog-headed god, Anubis, with the same mission.

Dogs can be incredible helpers when it comes to protection magic and magic dedicated to play and free-spiritedness. But in reality, getting a dog to behave in a particular way during a ritual or spell can be difficult. Dogs have free will. Instead try this: Sit down with your dog for a good petting session and meditate on color magic associations (see more on color magic in Chapter 4). You might even talk about this out loud to your dog. Then, take your dog to the pet store and let your dog pick out a collar, leash, or harness. Although dogs don't see colors the way humans do, the color your dog chooses can signal what kinds of magic you can do together.

CATS AND THE CRAFT

Cats have long been associated with witchcraft. Perhaps the connection dates back to the ancient Egyptians and the cat goddess Bastet. Cats are mysterious, aloof, and linked with magic and the moon. They seem to walk between the worlds, and at times it is as if they can see things we can't see. Some witches believe cats have the ability to predict the weather. If a witch sees a cat sleeping with its back to the fire, frost is coming. If a cat washes its ears, rain is on the way. Many witches keep cats as familiars, or magical helpers, because they are like embodiments of mysteries and hidden secrets. Even more so than dogs, cats have free will, and it is not realistic to expect cats to do anything they don't want to do. That said, a simple form of cat magic is a divination spell. Concentrate on a question. Write down the possible answers to your question on separate pieces of paper. Crumple the paper up into balls and throw them on the floor for your cat to play with. The paper ball the cat plays with most is the answer to your question.

FAMILIARS

Often, familiars are pets, but not always. Cats are the most traditional familiars, but familiars can be any creatures—rabbits, toads, snakes, dogs, birds, even insects. The most important thing is to remember you cannot force any creature to become a familiar. They have to choose you.

How to Attract a Familiar On a new moon, write down on a piece of paper the qualities you want in a familiar and place the paper under a candle in a holder. Light the candle, knowing the flame is projecting your request out to the universe. Be patient and keep an open mind.

Familiars will demonstrate their magical side by accompanying you when you are casting spells and holding your rituals. They watch you work with your magical tools, and show up to hang out during other witchy activities. Familiars lend a comforting presence, they guard over your magical work, and some witches believe familiars can even lend you knowledge and guide your witchcraft. You may dream about your familiar or feel that an animal is communicating with you. Take care of your familiar, and your familiar will take care of you.

Witchy Communities

Many kitchen witches choose the solitary path, working their magic alone. In earlier times, witches often lived apart from towns or cities, having little contact with other people except to offer healing and maybe some spells to those in need. Today, few witches cut themselves off from the world, and witches are more likely to live in the suburbs or a city than alone in the woods. However, you may decide not to practice your craft with other witches or become a member of an organized group. Perhaps you're a private person and prefer not to share this part of your life with other people. Maybe meeting regularly with a group doesn't suit your lifestyle. Or you might not have found a circle that's right for you. Some witches opt to be solitary for a period of time and then join a coven later, or vice versa. It's completely up to the individual. Neither path is better or worse, right or wrong.

But if you want to connect with other witches and like-minded folks, how do you go about it? If your town has a New Age shop, that's a good place to start. Otherwise, you might try talking to people at your local health food store. Unitarian Universalist and Unity churches tend to be spiritually inclusive and may have witches in their congregations. Yoga centers can be connection points too. Some colleges now offer courses in goddess-based spirituality and mythology. You'll also find plenty of information online about Wiccan, Pagan, and other groups in your area that share your philosophy and engage in practices that align with your beliefs and desires.

Kitchen witches tend to be independent folks who dislike hierarchy, dogma, and rigid structure. Some covens abide by specific traditions and ideologies—you may have heard of Dianic, Alexandrian, Gardnerian, or other types of witches. Of course, each coven is as unique as its members. Some are formal, others are relaxed. And there's no reason why you can't combine kitchen witchery with any other system.

A LITTLE BIT ABOUT COVENS

The word *coven* originated from the Latin terms *coventus* or *convenire*, which mean "assembly" or "agreement." By the mid-seventeenth century, the word had come to denote a witches' meeting or a local group of practicing witches. (*Covenant* comes from the same root.)

A Modern Description In her book *The Spiral Dance*, Starhawk gives an excellent description of a coven as "a Witch's support group, consciousness-raising group, psychic study center, clergy-training program, College of Mysteries, surrogate clan, and religious congregation all rolled into one."

Traditionally, covens comprised thirteen members. One theory says the number corresponds to the thirteen lunar months in the year, because lunar practices are an important part of witchcraft. Also, the moon's energy is feminine, and most witches in early times were women. Modern covens, however, may have any number of members, as few or as many as the group chooses and of any gender. Small groups offer more intimacy and personal interaction. Larger ones afford more opportunities for learning, sharing ideas and skills, and participating in a variety of activities.

Some witches join covens for the same reason people join churches: to find community and to share their beliefs with people who have similar ideologies, values, and purposes in life. A coven becomes your spiritual family. It's also fun to celebrate the sabbats and esbats, as well as personal events and special interests, with other witches. Working magic and performing rituals with a group can be an amazing experience, enabling you to raise more power than you could by yourself. My book *The Modern Guide to Witchcraft* discusses the pros and cons of covens, how you might benefit from joining one, how to find a group that's right for you, and a lot more.

A CIRCLE OF FRIENDS

A coven can be considered a circle of friends, although you may not like everyone in the group and might not have anything to do with them outside of the coven. If you decide a coven isn't right for you, but you still want to share your craft with other people, you could create a less formal circle. For many kitchen witches, this might be a comfortable way to go.

Maybe you already know several people whose ideas jive with your own or with whom you have common interests. Preparing meals and eating as a group is a natural way for kitchen witches to meet and enjoy being together, especially for esbats. *Esbat* refers to a lunar ritual that honors the Goddess, and they're usually held on the full or new moon. Depending on your circle, these gatherings can be as casual or elegant as you like. They may incorporate a lot of witchy workings or simply serve as a way for you and other witches to strengthen your friendship, support each other, and share spell recipes.

Your circle might also include people with whom you do business—from a New Age store, the local farmers' market, a bookstore that sells metaphysical books, a yoga center, and so on. If you dig around a bit, you may find like-minded individuals in your area.

Treating Your Market As a Sacred Space

Your busy, boisterous local supermarket may seem the antithesis of a holy place, and yet any place is a temple if you treat it that way. Today's supermarkets are the modern-day equivalent of the ancient marketplaces where our ancestors gathered for commerce and community and to share information. In earlier times, the market was a city or town's center, and it often featured a hearth where people made offerings to the gods and goddesses.

The idea of supermarkets, grocery stores, farm stands, and other places where you purchase your food as sacred spaces may not be totally foreign to kitchen witches. After all, food is their magical commodity, and they work their spells through the meals they prepare. They don't draw distinct lines that separate their spiritual practice from their everyday lives and activities. Grocery shopping also provides many opportunities to apply their beliefs.

Supermarket Shopping Game Ask kids to find an exotic food they don't recognize and challenge them to learn about its country of origin, history, mythology, and magical properties. Then find a recipe that includes the food and prepare it for the family.

As you peruse the aisles, feel gratitude for the abundance offered to you that isn't available in some parts of the world. As you select meat or fish to eat, remember the sacred hunt and give thanks to the creatures who sacrificed their lives that you may nourish yourself and your loved ones. Consider the individual energies of the various foods, not only their nutritional qualities but their magical ones as well. How can you incorporate certain fruits, vegetables, grains, and so on into your spells and rituals? (See Part 3 for more information.)

Pay It Forward Perhaps you've heard about the concept of "paying it forward." This is the practice of doing something good for other people, such as paying for their groceries even if you don't know them, as a way of expressing gratitude for having been the recipient of someone else's generosity. You could also help an elderly man who can't bend down to reach something on the bottom shelf or listen to a lonely woman in the pet-food aisle who wants to talk about her cat or dog. Even smiling at people can brighten their day.

The supermarket links you with people in your community as well as countless others you'll never know, including truck drivers, farmers, warehouse workers, people who harvest the food, and those who package it. It gives you an awareness of your interconnectedness with all life. If you bring your kids along with you, you'll have plenty of opportunities to teach them your values as well as practical lessons, such as how to choose quality items, how to understand Nutrition Facts labels, and where to find bargains.

The Magic of the Garden

The word *garden* brings to mind a place of peace, beauty, and happiness. In mythology and spiritual texts, the garden is often a symbol for paradise, for instance the biblical Garden of Eden. According to Greek myth, the goddess Hera's sacred Garden of the Hesperides produced apples that conferred immortality on the deities. The rare peaches that grew in the garden of the Chinese goddess Wangmu Niangniang achieved this same effect.

We still create gardens as holy sites that connect us with the divine realm. Islamic "paradise gardens," in which water is a key feature, are designed to be oases of hope, rest, and contemplation. The Hanging Gardens of Haifa, with its nineteen terraces and 1,500 steps that lead to the Shrine of the Bab at the top of a mountain, is the second holiest place on earth for Baha'is. Zen gardens are serene retreats where monks and laity go to meditate on the Buddha's teachings.

Growing your own food provides an opportunity to tune in to the entire growth cycle of any plant and connect with your practice on a deep level. Special relationships often exist between plants, animals, and humans, and you can learn about them through folklore.

THE THREE SISTERS GARDEN

A "Three Sisters" garden is created by growing corn, beans, and squash together. This technique comes from traditional Native American gardeners in several different parts of North America. Many Native American folktales have been woven around the Three Sisters—sisters who would never be apart from one another, sisters who should be planted together, eaten together, and celebrated together. But this is not just a lovely story. Native American farmers discovered through observation that these three plants actually helped and supported one another in the growing process.

The beans rely on the sturdy cornstalks around which to wrap their vines and reach up to the sun. In turn, the bean root systems provide important nutrients for the corn and squash. The broad leaves of the squash plants shade the ground, trapping much-needed moisture in the soil for all three plants. The Three Sisters garden creates a beautiful relationship among the three plants—each plant helps the others grow. This method is called "companion planting," and wise witches would do well to think about how they can learn from this example. For Native Americans, the meaning of the Three Sisters garden goes much deeper than just providing food. These gardens are representations of the physical and spiritual well-being of their people. The Three Sister spirits protect one another and, in doing so, protect and provide for the people.

Witches who grown their own food can play a similar role, casting their own spells to protect and provide for their families and communities, in harmony with the earth.

THE COMPELLING COMMUNITY GARDEN

Another spellbinding option for kitchen witches and their families is to start or get involved with a local community garden. A community garden is a neighborhood garden divided up into personal plots. Some gardens may have restrictions on what you can plant, but usually as long as they are legal to grow, any plants are fine. If you live in a city, where it can be hard to find yard space to foster a garden, a community garden might be a real blessing. Not only is this an amazing way to connect with others and learn how to produce your own food, you can grow your own magical herbs. Teaching children how to grow their own food is a surefire way to pass on magical traditions to the next generation and instill a sense of connection between young people and nature itself.

Garden-Variety Magic Some community gardens located in dense neighborhoods have waiting lists. If this is the case in your neighborhood, take advantage of the extra time you will have to plan your garden and think about timing your application with a season: spring for new beginnings, summer for achievement, fall for abundance and ancestor worship, or winter for establishing traditions.

Plant-savvy witches have some neat opportunities to connect with community through a community garden. If you are a member of a coven, this could be a place where your collective comes together to grow the plants and herbs that your magical group intends to use in your spells, rituals, and celebrations all year long. Imagine, for example, growing your own corn to harvest the sheaves for your corn dollies!

Showering in Your Garden In the Ringing Cedars book series, author Vladimir Megré writes about a woman named Anastasia who lives off the land in the remote Siberian wilderness. Descended from an ancient Vedic civilization, Anastasia has incredible mystical, magical, mental, and healing powers, plus a deep, intuitive connection with the natural world. She recommends showering in your garden so that the water/rain carries your essence to the plants. This allows them to receive information about your unique makeup and to grow in harmony with it, developing the qualities you need for good health.

Chapter 6

Kitchen Witchery for the Holidays

WITCHES OBSERVE THEIR OWN SET of holidays throughout the year in addition to the holidays celebrated in their native cultures. These holidays occur along what is known as the Wheel of the Year, and the number of celebrations varies by tradition but usually hovers between four and eight. Observing these holy days, or sabbats, is not required but is a magical way for kitchen witches to tune in to the energy of the seasons. In this chapter, you'll learn the basics of the eight pagan sabbats and some of the traditions observed during these holy days. You'll also learn about the classic foods and drinks pagans and witches concoct to celebrate their holidays. Kitchen witches will find ample opportunities to practice their craft in the framework of the Wheel of the Year.

Celebrating the Seasons

Many of the traditions connected to the sabbats go back thousands of years and reflect the mindsets of the people who held them dear. The sabbats harken to a time when people lived close to the land, in harmony with the seasons and cycles of the sun and moon. For folks who didn't have easy access to timekeeping devices like clocks and calendars, the sabbats were a way to give structure to the year and keep them on track to know when to plant, when to drive their cattle out to the fields, and when to pull in the harvest.

Four of the sabbats are linked to the movements of the sun. These are Ostara (spring equinox), Litha (summer solstice), Mabon (fall equinox), and Yule (winter solstice). The other four sabbats are Imbolc (February 1–2), Beltane (May 1), Lughnasad (August 1), and Samhain (October 31). It is important to remember that not all witches celebrate all the sabbats at the same time or in the same ways. For example, in December, while witches in the northern hemisphere are celebrating Yule and winter solstice, witches in the southern hemisphere are celebrating Litha and summer solstice. The Wheel of the Year customs are probably rooted in agricultural and animal-bearing rhythms. But witches don't know for sure, because the Christianizing of pagan communities throughout time erased much of the histories of these holidays. However, pagan traces are still felt in holy days like Easter, which falls between the springtime sabbats Ostara and Beltane every year. Dyed eggs, a practice at the heart of Easter, were sacred to many springtime goddesses.

Samhain ✳ October 31

The first sabbat is Samhain, pronounced "sow-in." *Samhain* is a Celtic word that means "summer's end" and reflects the Celtic worldview that summer ends at Samhain. This sabbat is celebrated in various forms around the world, sometimes under the name *Halloween* or *All Hallows'*

Eve, and focuses on honoring the dead and ancestors, with emphasis on traditions that bring you closer to loved ones who have passed on as well as the dwindling sunlight at this time of year.

For ancient Celtic pagans, this marked the end of the old year, the end of summer, and the beginning of the New Year and winter. This is also the official date for Celtic New Year. The tenth-century Irish myth *Tochmarc Emire* ("The Wooing of Emir") declares Samhain as the first of the seasonal festivals in the year. Ancient and modern Samhain celebrations are surprisingly similar: parties, feasting, wearing costumes, pulling pranks, and eating sweets—just like modern Halloween!

Samhain is a great time to flex your creativity muscles by building costumes and making masks. Of course, one of the most noteworthy Samhain traditions is carving pumpkins into jack-o'-lanterns and placing a candle inside to light the way for visiting spirits.

Jack-O'-Lantern History In America, pumpkins and jack-o'-lanterns are synonymous, but this vegetable is a relatively new addition to Samhain. Before this holiday made its way over the Atlantic, jack-o'-lanterns were carved from turnips. The practice of carving turnips and placing candles inside to ward off darkness goes back more than four hundred years.

BRING OUT YOUR DEAD

This sabbat can be a time for personal reflection on ancestors in addition to family members, community members, and pets who have moved on over the last year. Many pagans believe the divide between the world of the living and the dead grows thin at Samhain, making communication between the worlds easier. For this reason, divination and fortune-telling practices are common at this sabbat. Samhain provides an opportunity to meditate on a facet of life that no one has control over: death. Death is a spooky and uncomfortable subject for some folks, so people approach this holiday with a variety of attitudes, from somber to celebratory.

Your Samhain altar can include serious elements, like pictures of ancestors and friends who have passed and prayer candles, but it can also show a lighter side of this sabbat with bowls full of candy, Halloween masks, and, of course, a jack-o'-lantern. Samhain colors are black, white, silver, orange, and purple. You can also include elements of fall, like autumn leaves, dried flowers, pumpkins, squash, and nuts.

SAMHAIN FOODS AND BEVERAGES

One of the most familiar foods associated with Samhain is, of course, the pumpkin. So pumpkin everything is appropriate at this sabbat. Pumpkin pies, pumpkin bread, and even pumpkin spice lattes are festive at this time of year. Bobbing for apples is a traditional form of divination practiced at Samhain, and apple cider and caramel apples are also appropriate for this holy day. Other foods are raisins, mushrooms, pomegranates, and roast beef. And what would the holiday be without sweets? Candy and all manner of sweet treats are traditional foods for Samhain.

Yule ✳ December 21

Witches celebrate Yule on the winter solstice. The word *Yule* comes from the Old Norse word *jol*. The word *solstice* is Latin and means "sun" and "stand still." At the winter solstice, the sun appears to rise at the same place on the horizon three days in a row. Around this date in the northern hemisphere, people experience the shortest days of the year and the longest nights. The temperatures drop, and much of the natural world dies or goes into hibernation. After Yule, the days begin to grow longer, and the light of the sun begins to return. Yule rites celebrate the returning light of the sun and foster a sense of goodwill among the members of a family or community as the group gets ready to face the harsh conditions of winter together.

Yule embraces all things wintry, and pagan celebrations are the root of many modern Christmas traditions. You probably know that pagans honored trees (and still do). Evergreen trees that retain their leaves or needles during the long, harsh winter months remind us that life goes on even during the darkest times. The Christmas tradition of cutting down an evergreen tree, bringing it into the house, and decorating it came directly from pagan sources. Gift giving is another tradition from the past, possibly connected to the old Roman festival known as Saturnalia. Ancient pagans created handmade gifts and exchanged them with friends and loved ones. One of the most important aspects of Yuletide celebration is feasting. Early Norse people got together to feast and drink for twelve days straight, with plenty of naps in between.

The Yule Log The Yule log is a long-standing pagan tradition. A sacred piece of wood was burned, section by section, for twelve nights. A modern witch who doesn't have access to an outdoor firepit might choose to burn an oak log in the fireplace—remember to save a piece of the wood to include in next year's Yule fire. If you don't have a fireplace, you can set a special piece of wood on your altar or table, perhaps with holes drilled in it for candles.

Your Yule altar can include elements of rebirth, like images of a rising sun. Yule colors are red for the light of the returning sun, white for the frost-covered world, and green for the evergreens and the life force that sleeps under the snow. You can also add candles, evergreen boughs, mistletoe, wrapped presents, and handmade ornaments.

YULE FOODS AND BEVERAGES

Yuletide beverages take center stage at this time of year, with the most famous being a drink called wassail or grog. Many recipes for this drink have evolved throughout time and from region to region. Wassail is a warming drink filled with seasonal spices like cinnamon, ginger, nutmeg, clove, and allspice. Some recipes start with a base of apple cider and fruit juice, and others use a base of red wine. You may want to serve a boozy and a nonalcoholic version of this drink. The mix is kept warm over low heat and served all day to visiting friends, family, and those seeking refuge from the cold weather. Provide a little snack alongside a steaming cup of wassail, like a piece of cinnamon toast, a dumpling, a baked apple, or another simple treat.

Other Yuletide foods include bread pudding, roasted nuts, and gingerbread cookies. The Jewish festival of Hanukkah often overlaps Yule, and many folks leave room on the menu for potato latkes.

Imbolc * February 1–2

The next sabbat in the Wheel of the Year is Imbolc, pronounced "ihm-bolk." Also known as Candlemas, this sabbat is often dedicated to the Irish goddess Brigid (see Chapter 2 for more information on her), although you could honor any god or goddess of the hearth at this time of year. The word *Imbolc* means "in the belly" and recognizes the creativity that resides in each of us. Artists often depict Brigid stirring a cauldron, a witch's tool that corresponds to feminine power and fertility of the mind as well as the body.

At Imbolc, the weather is often cold and frosty and the days, though lengthening, are still relatively short. Many Imbolc celebrations are centered around reigniting your creativity, energy, and passion for life after the long darkness of midwinter.

Many witches make candles at this sabbat as a way to honor the returning light. Making candles can be a fun way to spend an otherwise dreary day indoors. Imbolc celebrations may include a moment during which someone wears a crown of candles, but you can also make an Imbolc wreath as a table centerpiece to hold your Imbolc candles. (See Part 4 for information on making your own candles.) Even if you don't fashion your own, you'll want to burn candles on your altar and elsewhere in your home on this sabbat.

Another name for this sabbat is *Oimelc*, which means "ewe's milk" and refers to all the lactating animals having their first round of babies at this time. Milk is traditionally a symbol of both abundance and purification. During Imbolc, witches begin to clear out their gardens for the coming growth season of spring.

One popular holiday that may be connected to Imbolc is Groundhog Day. German immigrants brought this festival with them when they came to America, although originally they waited for a badger to show up. If the badger poked out of its burrow and saw its shadow, it promptly retreated and hid for another six weeks, signaling a longer winter. If it did not see a shadow and stayed above ground, winter would wrap up soon.

Another important holiday that often runs concurrent to Imbolc is Lunar New Year, a festival celebrated in different variations by many Asian cultures. This holy date is observed by billions of people around the planet. Lunar New Year is celebrated with fireworks, feasting with loved ones, and exchanging good wishes for the New Year.

Your Imbolc altar can include symbols of purification; your witch's broom, stuff to donate, even cleaning tools. You might also want to burn incense or sage on your altar for cleansing and clearing. Imbolc colors are brown, black, white, and silver. You can also include white candles and flowers that are in season, like daffodils, hyacinths, crocuses, and other flowering bulbs.

IMBOLC FOODS AND BEVERAGES

Traditional fare for Imbolc often includes dairy ingredients, especially milk. Creams, cheeses, and eggs are all popular ingredients at Imbolc. Try your hand at making your own butter on this holiday. Honey and homemade breads are also important. Pancakes and crepes, too, are traditional foods at Imbolc. Make a wish while flipping your Imbolc pancakes. Another time-honored dish at Imbolc is mashed potatoes (with lots of cream and butter, of course). Everyone in the family should take a turn mashing the potatoes to make sure there is a good mix of magical energy in the dish.

Kitchen witches who want to honor the Lunar New Year might serve shrimp, oranges and tangerines, spring rolls, pork belly, baby bok choy, and dumplings, each representing wealth, good health, and happiness.

Ostara ✳ March 21

Ostara marks the official start of spring and end of winter. This sabbat falls on the spring equinox each year. The equinox is a moment when day and night are of equal length. Because of this astronomical event, balance and equilibrium are a big part of the symbolism for Ostara. After this moment, every day grows longer, the earth begins to wake up from winter, and flowers and plants begin to bloom. We see this natural event depicted in the stories of the deities Osiris, Mithra, Jesus, and Persephone returning from the lands of the dead and bringing new life with them.

Rebirth and new beginnings are important symbols for this sabbat. Budding plants, babies (of all species), and all new things are connected to Ostara. One powerful way to bring in the energy of new beginnings is a deep spring cleaning of your kitchen, home, or yard to get ready for the coming months of activity. This is a customary time for witches and pagans to start their magical gardens for the year.

For thousands of years many religions and cultures have celebrated the spring equinox. Jewish Passover happens around this time of year, as does the Christian tradition of Easter. The Persian New Year, Nowruz, starts on this date too. Eggs dyed bright red to symbolize the returning sun are one of the central features of its celebration.

Eggs As New Life Eggs are an important feature at Ostara because they symbolize the beginning of life. Countless forms of life on earth start out in an egg, including birds, mammals, fish, amphibians, reptiles, and insects. The "cosmic egg" is a symbol that's often used to represent the birth of the universe.

EOSTRE AND EASTER

Ostara possibly gets its name from the goddess Eostre. Eostre is a Teutonic goddess whose name means "of the rising dawn," in reference to the season of spring and the increasing light. Ancient pagans worshipped her with flowers, eggs, and rabbits. A historian named the Venerable Bede first recorded stories of this goddess and her springtime traditions in the 700s C.E. while on a trip across Europe documenting pagan traditions for the Catholic Church. The Church tried to change the pagan focus from Eostre to the resurrection story of Jesus, but ancient pagans clung tightly to their traditions. Eventually, the Church gave up and changed the name of their springtime festival to Easter, in an attempt to unite the two holy days.

Your Ostara altar can include elements of spring and birth: dyed eggs, plans for your garden, and baby plants. Ostara colors are pastel tones. You can also include nature's expressions of the changing season, like branches from flowering trees such as cherry, apple, or dogwood.

OSTARA FOODS AND BEVERAGES

Eggs are at the center of Ostara celebrations, and not just for dyeing. Decorating eggs with colors and magical designs goes back thousands of years (see Part 3 for more information on eggs). Deviled eggs will likely be on your Ostara menu, and maybe a tasty omelet seasoned with spring onions. Other classic Ostara dishes are lamb, fish, ham, and caviar. Braided breads are an Ostara tradition, as are hot cross buns. Eggnog is often associated with Yule and wintertime traditions, but it is equally appropriate for Ostara. This is also a great time to start making meads with honey and young spring flowers.

Beltane ✱ May 1

To the ancient Celtic pagans, Beltane marked the high point of the spring season and celebrated the surging life force on earth. Virility, fertility, and sexual energy are at the forefront of this sabbat's symbolism.

Some historians think Beltane may have acquired its name from the Celtic fire god Bel (aka Belenos, Belinus, Beli Mawr). But it is just as likely to be derived from a word meaning "balefire," as balefires or bonfires are a central theme at Beltane. These fires had to be built from nine sacred types of wood, and the fires themselves had to be started through friction, like rubbing two sticks together. Livestock were driven between the Beltane fires for purification, healing, and protection. Folks took turns jumping the bonfires so they could be purified and protected as well. Witches brought glowing coals from the Beltane fires back to their houses to relight their home fires and ensure good fortune in the home and safety for the new life coming into the world. Ashes from the Beltane fires were used to bless people and animals and were scattered over the lands to fertilize and protect the crops.

THE MAYPOLE

Perhaps the best-known Beltane custom is dancing around the Maypole. The phallic symbolism of the Maypole is obvious, and the erection of the pole is a form of sympathetic magic that represents the god's climbing power. To create your own Maypole, find or buy a long, straight length of wood. Weave a wreath of flowers and attach it to the pole so that it encircles the top. This is a symbol of the sexual union between goddess and god energy. Tie several multicolored ribbons to the flower wreath. The ribbons should be twice the length of the pole. For example, if your pole is 10 feet tall, the ribbons should be at least 20 feet long. Erect the pole by securing the base in a hole in the ground or in a 5-gallon bucket filled with rocks. Celebrants should assemble in two circles around the pole. Each grasps a ribbon, and as music plays the circles move in opposite directions—one clockwise, the other counterclockwise. The dancers bob up and down, holding their ribbons above their neighbors' heads or ducking under the ribbons in turn to create a colorful braid down the pole, thus symbolically weaving the energies of the goddess and god together.

Your Beltane altar can include symbols of fertility and sensuality; anything that feels sexy and sensual can go on your Beltane altar. Beltane colors are party colors, like hot pink, turquoise, grass green, and lemon yellow. You can also include gardening tools, bouquets of seasonal flowers, or a miniature Maypole.

BELTANE FOODS AND BEVERAGES

Given all the sexy energy of Beltane, it should come as no surprise that aphrodisiac foods are particularly popular during this sabbat. The word *aphrodisiac* comes from the goddess Aphrodite, who is credited with planting the first pomegranate tree, so pomegranates are at the top of the list. Strawberries, cherries, and raspberries all honor the goddess at Beltane. Rhubarb represents masculine energy. The tall, stiff red stalks honor the surging god energy, making it a favorite food at Beltane. With its effervescent bubbles and history of being the drink of choice at celebrations, champagne is the spirit of Beltane in a bottle. And don't forget the chocolate, one of the most well-known aphrodisiac foods.

Litha * June 21

The sun reaches its apex at the summer solstice, which is also known as Litha or midsummer. This sabbat celebrates the height of the sun's power and influence. On this date, people in the northern hemisphere experience the longest day and shortest night. To underscore this effect, many pagans hold their Litha celebrations during the day, starting at noon, when the sun is directly overhead.

Solar symbols, light, fire, and heat are all fundamental features of Litha festivities. As at Beltane, celebrants may build roaring bonfires on this sabbat to bless and protect themselves, their animals, and their lands.

Another name for Litha is Gathering Day. Many witches and pagans see Litha as the most sacred time to gather the herbs they will use in their magic for the rest of the year. This is because the sun has infused the plants with its energy at the height of its powers. Before that power begins to wane or fade, witches want to gather as much of this magic as is possible.

Ethical Harvesting Always approach your harvesting with respect and ask the plant for permission to harvest it. Sit quietly for a moment and listen for a response. Follow a one-in-four rule—for every four plants you find, harvest only one, to make sure there's some left for next year. Never ingest any plant you cannot identify.

This gathering work is so sacred that witches often use a special knife just for harvesting herbs. Witches who have planted their own herbs begin to reap the rewards of that labor. It is also traditional to gather wildflowers at this time and dry them.

Litha is also a time to strengthen family bonds, whether that is your genetic relations or chosen family. Family reunions and handfastings (pagan marriages) are a time-honored practice at Litha. Research your family name and lineage, learn about your ancestry, and wear your family colors with pride.

The fairy folk may also show up at witches' Litha rites. Many pagans leave out a small dish with honey, water, butter, milk, wine, and bread as a gift and a type of bribe for the fairies, who are especially active and mischievous at this time of year.

Your Litha altar can include symbols of light and heat: images of the sun or fires and candles. Litha colors are bright summer colors, like cobalt blue, bright orange, sunny yellow, white, and rainbows. If you harvest herbs at this sabbat, make sure to hang them over your altar to charge them as they dry (but make sure you hang them away from any candles).

LITHA FOODS AND BEVERAGES

Edibles that feature herbs of all types are good choices for Litha. Vermouth infused with flowers, herbs, seeds, and spices; lemonade with strawberries; and chamomile tea all capture the sunny essence of Litha. Sage-encrusted pork, rosemary chicken, lavender cheesecake, blueberry pie, lemon cookies, peach cobbler, and orange blossom honey butter slathered on fresh biscuits are all great Litha dishes. Summer squash and zucchini are in season at this time, so bring on the zucchini bread. Spicy foods especially honor the heat of the sun during this sabbat. Add marigolds, honeysuckle, hibiscus, sunflowers (and sunflower seeds), nasturtiums, dandelions, and other edible flowers to your holiday salads. And, of course, with all the flowers in bloom, this is another perfect sabbat for bottling your own mead. A bottle of mead takes about six months to age properly, so mead bottled at Litha will be ready in time for Yule gifting.

Lughnasad * August 1

The sabbat Lughnasad gets its name from the Irish god Lugh, whose name literally means "shining one." Lugh is a god of competition, warriors, and crafting skill. Modern Lughnasad traditions are a remnant of ancient Gaelic pagan harvest festivals celebrating the first harvests of the year. Great gatherings held for weeks on end marked this time of year, with ritual competitions and magical games at the center of the merrymaking.

This sabbat is also known as First Harvest. Pagans venerated the first ears of grain that ripened, and it was good luck to be the one picked to harvest them. These first harvests were then baked into loaves of bread that were broken up and shared with everyone working the harvest. Crumbs were scattered around the corners of the house and property to ensure protection and prosperity for everyone.

LOAF MASS

Another name for this sabbat is *Lammas*, which means "loaf mass." May grains are ready for harvest at this time of year, and sacred breads play an essential role in Lughnasad ceremonies. Try your hand at baking bread for this sabbat, especially if you've never done it before.

Corn ripens at this time as well. Peruvian people celebrate the corn harvest with a parade. Elders pass out handfuls of corn kernels, which folks tuck into their pockets to either scatter in their fields or save for fertility spells. Pagans dry the husks of corn from the first harvests and use them to make corn dollies. These dollies represent the Goddess, and they will be placed back in the ground during Imbolc, when planting starts all over again, connecting the energy from one cycle to the next.

Your Lughnasad altar can include symbols of the first harvest, like homemade loaves of bread and ears of corn. If you make corn dollies, be sure to place them on your altar for blessing. Lughnasad colors are gold, red, burnt orange, and deep yellows. You can also include fiery objects such as candles and hot peppers.

LUGHNASAD FOODS AND BEVERAGES

Breads and foodstuffs made with grains are the most important edibles at Lughnasad. Anything that features oats, wheat, rye, barley, or rice is sacred at this time. This includes malted milkshakes, beer, whiskey, sake, and bourbon. Corn bread, popcorn, and polenta are all perfect for Lughnasad. Seasonal fruits and vegetables like blackberries ripen during this time, so take advantage and make blackberry pies or blackberry wine. Bilberries, currants, tomatoes, gooseberries, onions, garlic, turnips, and fennel are all magical foods for Lughnasad. Take the kids to a local farm to pick up your produce. Many items will likely have been harvested that morning. During warm summer weather, enjoy outdoor barbecues and have fun hanging out with friends, family members, and neighbors.

Mabon ❋ September 21

During the sabbat Ostara, the spring equinox, there is a moment of balance before heading into the light half of the year. At the fall equinox marked by the sabbat Mabon, pronounced "maa-bun," that moment of balance returns before heading into the dark half of the year. On one hand, the light is dying; on the other hand, the earth provides incredible opulence and bounty.

The daylight begins to dwindle, the nights get longer, and pagans know winter is only a few short months away. Pagans often take this time to reflect on and thank their ancestors, who may be coming back to visit at Samhain.

Yet, even as the sun's light begins to diminish, the rich yield of the yearly harvest arrives. Mabon is the central abundance sabbat of the year. Feasting, generosity, giving thanks, and celebrating all that has been gained over the year are at the heart of Mabon rites.

The grape harvest in particular held importance to many pagan communities of old. Ancient Greeks and Romans held festivals at this time of year dedicated to Dionysus, Bacchus, and other "gods of the vine." Wine is a powerful magical element in countless religious practices. But it wasn't just about getting tipsy. Grapevines are quite sturdy and can often take the place of rope. You can make a grapevine garland that will last all year by simply soaking vines in water until they are pliable, weaving them into the shape you want, and then letting them dry. With a little ingenuity and seasonal decorations, your grapevine wreath can be the base of all your sabbat wreaths.

Share the Bounty Mabon is a season to celebrate abundance, and one of the most holy ways you can do that is to volunteer your time at a soup kitchen, outreach center, or shelter. Commit to extending your bounty to the community around you and know that you honor your ancestors and the deities through this work.

If there was one symbol that encapsulated the spirit of this sabbat, it would be the cornucopia, or horn of plenty, the universal sign of abundance. Modern pagans often call this holiday "Witches' Thanksgiving," and some even move their yearly Thanksgiving dinners to this date.

Your Mabon altar can include symbols of abundance: bowls full of fruit and vegetables, piles of coins, or even a cornucopia. Mabon colors are earth tones, like brown, russet, olive, mustard, and maroon. You can also include seasonal plants, like autumn leaves, dried flowers, acorns, nuts, and seeds.

MABON FOODS AND BEVERAGES

Because grapes come into season at this time of year, grape juice, wine, port, cognac, and grappa—an Italian drink made from the leftovers of wine making—are all seasonally magical. Apples, too, are popular Mabon foods and you should enjoy them in as many ways as possible, from apple butter to apple pie to baked apples to apple cider. Seasonal vegetables like squash, corn, beets, and beans can also be part of your Mabon feast. Nut harvests come in too, and walnuts, almonds, hazelnuts, peanuts, and pecans feature prominently in pies, stuffings, and other treats both sweet and savory. If you and your loved ones eat meat, consider serving roast duck, goose, or turkey at your Mabon supper.

Part 3

An Encyclopedia of Magical Edibles

The recipe for history's best-known witch's brew can be found in Shakespeare's play *Macbeth*, and it includes such creepy ingredients as eye of newt and toe of frog. However, according to Darcy Larum writing for *Dave's Garden*, these are ordinary substances. In bygone days, witches and other herbalists often substituted macabre words to keep the contents of their spells secret—and perhaps because "eye of newt" sounds a lot more exotic (and powerful) than plain old mustard seed, which is its common name. Modern kitchen witches still use some of the herbs *Macbeth*'s trio did, they just dispense with the unusual names. In fact, most tend to work with everyday ingredients they can find in the supermarket or New Age store—or better yet, ones they've grown in their own gardens.

Everything in this world emits energy of some kind, and everything has a unique energy "signature." Plants are living entities, and each contains distinctive qualities you draw on in spells for love, prosperity, protection, health, and more. As a kitchen witch, stock up on herbs and spices that not only add flavor to the dishes you make but infuse your food with magical properties. This part explains the properties of familiar herbs, fruits, vegetables, and grains, and recommends ways you can use them in your spellwork.

As a general rule, dried botanicals have longer shelf lives and their effects last longer too. However, their actions are slower and less intense. Use them in spells you intend to last for a while. Fresh plant materials act more quickly, and their energy is livelier. Use them in spells to materialize faster but that needn't last a long time.

Allspice

This versatile spice encourages good luck in many forms. Witches use its berries or the ground powder in spells for prosperity and abundance, career success, and personal empowerment. Ruled by Mars, the planet of assertiveness and vitality, allspice can increase the power of a spell or speed up the action of your workings. In addition to cooking with it, you can put the spice in talismans and charm bags—and then carry them in your pocket or purse to attract good fortune. Include allspice in a potpourri with other prosperity herbs, such as cloves or cinnamon, and set the blend in your office to boost creativity and productivity.

As its name suggests, allspice has many uses and is a popular culinary flavoring. Native to Central America and the West Indies, particularly Jamaica (it's sometimes called Jamaican pepper), it was brought to Europe by Columbus. Allspice adds interest to fish and meat dishes as well as vegetables, fruits, soups, and beverages. As an herbal remedy, allspice brewed in a tea aids digestion and can help calm nausea.

Aloe

Since ancient times, witches have served as healers in their communities, and they relied on the magical properties of plants for their remedies. Aloe has a long history as a medicinal plant, especially in hot climates, where healers used it to treat burns, rashes, insect bites, cuts, acne, sores, and other skin ailments. It's even mentioned in ancient Egyptian writings as a plant of immortality and was applied during embalming.

Kitchen witches consider aloe to be a powerful protection plant that can safeguard them against accidents in the kitchen—and if they do suffer a burn while cooking, aloe gel can soothe the wound. Our ancestors positioned aloe plants near the entrances to their homes as protection charms against evil forces and disease. They also rubbed the slimy juice from the plant on doorjambs and windowsills to repel unwanted entities and to prevent injuries in the home.

Chopped or crushed aloe leaves, when added to soups, salads, salsas, vegetable dishes, or juices, invite good health and overall well-being. The succulent's juice and pulp also provide relief for stomach ailments, ulcers, digestive complaints, heartburn, and intestinal problems. Use aloe gel to soften and rejuvenate dry skin, take the fire out of sunburn, and minimize wrinkles. The plant can also play a role in spells for beauty and youthfulness.

Try enjoying a few ounces of refreshing, organic aloe juice before eating breakfast. This cleansing drink will balance your digestion and lets you begin your day on a pleasant note.

Angelica

Angelica's purification properties make it ideal for cleansing sacred spaces and areas where rituals will be performed. During the Middle Ages, herbalists linked it with the archangel Michael and believed it offered protection against the plague and evil entities. Then, and now, the herb gave seekers a tool to communicate with the angels and to solicit divine assistance. If you want to gain guidance from the spirit realm, incorporate this herb into your cooking.

Angelica's root serves as a flavoring for candies, baked goods, and other sweets; its seeds are used in alcoholic beverages including gin and vermouth. You can also simmer angelica in a pot of water (or in your cauldron), then strain out the plant material and pour the herb-infused water into a ritual bath before engaging in a ceremony or magical working. Angelica washes away physical and psychic imbalances, leaving you ready to receive divine inspiration and direction. You can also cleanse magic tools, crystals, and other objects with water prepared with angelica. If you fear contamination from a pathogen or a malevolent force, put angelica in an amulet and carry it with you, or sprinkle the dried herb on your doorstep to ward off illness.

Anise

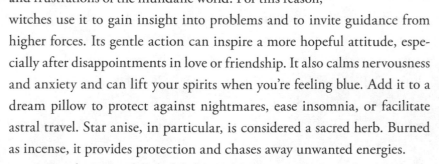

When doing tarot or rune readings or another type of divination, set a bowl of pretty star anise nearby. This fragrant herb improves psychic vision and helps you see beyond the narrow limitations and frustrations of the mundane world. For this reason, witches use it to gain insight into problems and to invite guidance from higher forces. Its gentle action can inspire a more hopeful attitude, especially after disappointments in love or friendship. It also calms nervousness and anxiety and can lift your spirits when you're feeling blue. Add it to a dream pillow to protect against nightmares, ease insomnia, or facilitate astral travel. Star anise, in particular, is considered a sacred herb. Burned as incense, it provides protection and chases away unwanted energies.

Aniseed gives a delightful flavor to cakes, cookies, and other sweet baked goods. It's also the special ingredient in Mexican wedding cookies and encourages happy relationships. Brewed in a tea, it relieves colds, congestion, and coughs—its antiviral properties can help protect against viruses. Herbal healers also recommend it for digestive complains, minor stomach cramps, and nausea. Folk medicine says that nursing mothers can ingest anise to increase milk production.

Apple

To kitchen witches, the apple has many positive con- notations. For starters, it's a symbol of love. Apples are also considered good luck (just look what the iconic fruit did for the technology giant). Mabon, the sabbat pagans celebrate at the fall equinox, is sometimes thought of as an apple harvest rite because it occurs at the time when apples are ready to pick. Witches also link apples with longevity and protection—apple blossoms are said to confer immortality. If you cut an apple in half and look at the configuration of the seeds inside, you'll notice they form a pentagram. And, of course, you've heard the saying "An apple a day keeps the doctor away." That's because apples represent good health.

Witch altars are often piled high with apples for the sabbat Samhain, as apples are often thought of as a food for the dead. Other witches bury apples at Samhain for the same reason. In Celtic myth, a bough that had all three phases of the apple's growth cycle—buds, flowers, and ripened fruit—was called the Silver Bough and was thought to be a type of magical charm that would let the bearer pass into the lands of the deities and the underworld.

Artichoke

The artichoke's many layers, which you peel away while eating it, symbolize peeling away your own outer layers of uncertainty, defensiveness, and artifice. Thus, the kitchen witch may eat or serve this vegetable to someone else who's engaged in self-examination or who wants to get to the core of a situation. Artichokes can also help you muster the courage to speak your own truth. Historically, the artichoke's spiky parts have been used in protection spells—lay the thistles at the corners of your home to ward off unwanted entities.

A type of thistle, artichokes have been revered for centuries for their ability, when eaten, to enhance male libido and sexual prowess. It's said that England's King Henry VIII consumed huge amounts of this vegetable. This may be an example of sympathetic magic, for the stalk, with its showy flower, has a phallic appearance. Some astrologers connect it with the planet Venus, which makes it a good choice for love spells (Venus rules love and relationships). Others suggest the plant falls into Mars's domain (the planet of sexuality, courage, and assertiveness). Either way, artichokes have long been considered an aphrodisiac.

Asparagus

This springtime vegetable is a perfect food to serve at a Beltane ritual meal on May 1. Its phallic shape makes it a natural choice to use in symbolic magic for male virility, desire, and sexual prowess and for love spells in general. Serve this natural aphrodisiac to increase the heat in a relationship that's lost its luster or to spark passion in a new romance.

According to astrologers, asparagus is ruled by the planet Jupiter, which governs growth, expansion, success, higher knowledge, and long-distance travel. Kitchen witches can incorporate asparagus into meals designed to support these areas or to bring increase in general.

The ancient Greeks attributed asparagus to their love goddess Aphrodite. The plant was also said to be a favorite of France's Sun King, Louis XIV, and his wife. And because it's one of the first vegetables to poke its head above the frozen ground in the spring, asparagus represents rebirth and renewal. Thus, it often shows up on Easter menus not only because it's in season then, but for its symbolic value.

Avocado

The avocado's shape, with the single large seed in the center, clearly resembles the womb. Sympathetic magic, therefore, connects this fruit with fertility and creativity. If you want to get pregnant, tap avocado's rich symbolism by including a seed in a talisman for that purpose. The Aztecs considered avocados aphrodisiacs and believed eating them stimulated sexual desire. Astrologers give rulership of the fruit to the planet Venus, which governs love and relationships, so you may choose to use avocados in spells to attract a new lover or to increase affectionate feelings and caring in an existing partnership.

Avocado's association with fruitfulness makes it beneficial in spells for growth and abundance of all kinds. Artistic people may find it also stimulates their creative process, for it supports children of the mind as well as of the body. Carve the seed with runes or other images that relate to your objective, then carry or wear the seed as a good luck charm (if you do this while the seed is still fresh and relatively soft, it's easier than if you wait until it dries out and hardens).

Avocados also offer a number of health advantages. They're rich in many vitamins, minerals, and healthy fats that promote good skin and a strong immune system.

Banana

In the same way sympathetic magic likens the avocado's shape to the womb and female fertility, it links the banana's obvious phallic symbolism with male sexuality. Therefore, it can behoove kitchen witches to use bananas in spells to increase a man's fertility or to arouse his lust.

Want to encourage passion in a romantic relationship? How about serving a lover (or potential partner) a banana split? This favorite dessert combines the sexy implications of the banana with the loving energy of chocolate, plus the comfort, sweetness, and feminine sensuality of ice cream (it's ruled by the Moon). Sprinkle on some walnuts, which represent new opportunities and fertility. Add some ripe, red, luscious, heart-shaped strawberries (one of Venus's favorite foods), and you've got the makings of an ideal love charm.

In India, bananas are prized and included in many celebratory meals as well as everyday diets. Native to Southeast Asia, they're some of the oldest cultivated fruits. Alexander the Great is credited with bringing bananas to the Middle East because he liked them so much. Bananas are not only yellow skinned, they also come in a variety of colors, including purple, red, and green—colors the kitchen witch may look to for symbolism in spellcraft.

Barley

In astrology, Venus, the planet of love and relationships, rules barley. Therefore, kitchen witches can use it in spells for love, domestic harmony, and congenial relationships. Throw barley at a wedding instead of rice to wish the new couple a happy marriage. Include pearl barley in talismans to encourage romance. At Yule, serve a hearty stew with barley in it (and seasoned with some of the love-related spices listed in this part) to bring love and happiness in the New Year.

Since ancient times, barley has been connected with strength and endurance, perhaps because it's rich in protein and has no cholesterol—though, of course, our ancestors didn't understand these things the way we do now. Roman gladiators ate it to give them an advantage in the arena. Folklore tells that barley can ease physical and emotional pain. Tie three stalks of barley together and envision your pain contained in the knot. Toss the barley into a stream or river; as the water carries the grain away, visualize it washing away your suffering too.

Barley is also a main ingredient in beer and scotch—it's been used for thousands of years in brewing beer, perhaps the oldest alcoholic beverage known to humankind. So the next time you toast a glass of your favorite brew, visualize attracting love, vitality, or whatever else you wish for.

Basil

Witches consider basil one of the most effective all-around protection herbs. Hang dried basil leaves above doorways to safeguard your home. Add dried, crushed leaves to an amulet pouch and carry it on your person to protect you wherever you go. Simmer a bunch of fresh basil in a cauldron or pot, then strain out the herb and pour the infused water around your home to ward off harm. You can also brush basil water on doorsteps or window frames to deter intruders.

Cultivated for five thousand years, this popular culinary herb is native to Southeast Asia, India, and central Africa, but cooks in many parts of the world, especially Italy, prize it for its wonderful fragrance and flavor. Basil enhances soups, stews, sauces, and salads—plus, it's easy to grow. Consider keeping a small pot on a windowsill in your kitchen so you can have fresh leaves at the ready. Herbal healers use it to improve digestion, settle an upset stomach, calm motion sickness, relieve anxiety, and ease symptoms of the common cold.

Bay (Bay Laurel)

In spellworking, bay leaves enhance success, fame, status, and reputation and bring honor. They were sacred to the Greek sun god Apollo. Add them to a talisman or charm bag to attract good fortune and abundance. Carry a few leaves in your pocket to help you win a contest or get a promotion at work. Bay laurel also encourages wisdom and expanded sight. The priestess of the oracle at Delphi is said to have chewed the leaves to inspire visions—you may choose to nibble on one before engaging in divination. Use them in potions to strengthen your intuition or as an aid to lucid dreaming and astral travel.

A widely used kitchen herb, bay leaves find their way into many a beef dish, including stews, soups, and roasts. They also have a place in Greek and Italian cooking. Tap bay laurel's purifying power by burning the leaves to cleanse an area after an illness or an emotional disturbance. You can also soak a small laurel branch in water, then asperge a person, object, or area prior to performing a ritual or spell.

Beans

With over four hundred varieties of beans, it is hard to explain the magical properties of all of them, but here are some: Sweet tonka beans help in love spells. Black beans can help you overcome obstacles and bring clarity when you need to make decisions. Green beans attract wealth. Navy beans increase strength. Red kidney beans encourage love and passion. Scatter a combination of dried beans around your home to ward off harmful spirits. Consider a bean's color, shape, and size and other characteristics in order to determine what magic properties it contains.

A staple in the diets of people the world over, beans are some of the most commonly eaten foods throughout the planet. They're also some of the most diverse crops and are among the oldest cultivated plants, grown for at least six thousand years. Beans have long been connected with magic—remember the fairy tale "Jack and the Beanstalk"?

In Sicily, fava beans enjoy almost holy status. During the Middle Ages, a drought crippled Sicily's crops; only the tough fava bean survived and saved the people from starvation. All these years later, fava beans are placed on altars and prepared in celebratory meals on St. Joseph's Day in gratitude.

Beet

The red juice of the beet has made it a favorite substitute for blood for witches who don't feel like opening a vein for a magical working. You can also use it instead of ordinary ink to write down magic spells in your Book of Shadows or to pen secret contracts. The connection between beets and blood dates back thousands of years to the ancient Romans, who believed the vegetable healed wounds and boosted stamina. Hippocrates, the "father of modern medicine," recommended eating beets to cleanse the blood.

Because the color red is associated with passion and sexuality, beet juice can be a good choice for written affirmations, incantations, and other spells related to love. Then, there's the sugar connection—beets are the source of a significant portion of the world's sugar, and their sweetness lends itself to spells for love and romance. The early Greeks theorized that the love goddess Aphrodite ate beets to enhance her beauty.

Beet juice also makes a pretty red dye for Ostara eggs. Simply chop a couple beets and boil them in water with vinegar and salt, then strain out the beets and let the water cool. Submerge hard-boiled eggs in the red water until they reach the depth of color you desire.

Black Pepper

No, black pepper isn't something you use to work black magic. Pepper's stimulating energy speeds the action of spells and brings quick results, whatever your intention. Try not to use powdered commercial black pepper for spells; it's too insipid. Instead, get a pepper grinder and grind fresh peppercorns for your workings.

Ruled by Mars, black pepper's energy is assertive, intense, competitive, and fast acting. Use it to spark courage, confront challenges and danger, or protect what's yours. It's a warrior's spice. Although it bears similarities to red pepper (cayenne), black pepper's influence is more focused and long-lasting. For example, if you need a power boost for a project that will take a while to come to fruition, black pepper is a better choice than red. Burn black peppercorns on charcoal discs to eliminate the unwanted effects of an adversary's actions so you can take control of the future. You can also sprinkle black pepper at the entrances to your home or business to repel unwanted intruders (physical or psychic).

In terms of cooking, black pepper brings out the flavors of meats, poultry, eggs, cheese, potatoes and other vegetables, and, well, pretty much everything—even strawberries, melons, and pears.

Blackberry

Like strawberries and raspberries, blackberries have connections to love and relationships. Blackberry tea sweetened with honey has long been considered an aphrodisiac. One way a kitchen witch can win a prospective lover's heart is to bake the object of your affection a blackberry pie and top it with vanilla ice cream. Serve it at the harvest festival Lughnasad on August 1 to bring prosperity as well.

Blackberry bushes, however, are studded with thorns, which may symbolize the thorny challenges that often accompany romantic relationships. You can use this spiky physical property to your advantage in protection spells to safeguard your loved ones. Weave a wreath with blackberry, rowan, and other plants known for their protective energies and hang it on the front door to your home. Put dried blackberry leaves in an amulet to keep someone you love safe. Pick the fruit during the waning moon and let it dry in the sunshine, then scatter the dried berries around your dwelling. If you live in an apartment, place dried blackberries in a bowl along with basil and rosemary and set the bowl near the entrance to your home.

Folklore tells us fairies like to shelter in blackberry patches. If you work with the fae, you may want to leave offerings of honey and home-baked sweets amid blackberry brambles to win their favor.

Blueberry

Long valued by kitchen witches for their ability to calm the emotions and instill tranquility, blueberries attract peace and harmony to your home. If you or someone you love is undergoing a lot of stress, bake blueberry muffins or a blueberry pie to encourage feelings of love, comfort, and support. With a fork, poke symbols or words that represent your intentions into the pie's top crust.

Blueberries combine well with other berries, not only in baked goods but also in juices and teas. Their soothing properties complement the loving energies of strawberries and raspberries to promote congeniality in romantic relationships. At breakfast, top your cereal with fresh blueberries and eat them to start the day on a peaceful note. Dry blueberries and add them to potpourris to clear away discordant energies in your home or workplace.

Chock-full of nutrients and antioxidants, blueberries have long been prized for their ability to turn back time, encouraging youthful beauty and vitality—for, as you know, stress is one of the biggest contributors to aging and poor health. Contemporary studies show blueberries can also help reduce levels of "bad" cholesterol and benefit your heart, perhaps one reason early kitchen witches linked them with health and happiness.

Brussels Sprouts

Like other green vegetables (although they also come in a purple variety), Brussels sprouts are linked with prosperity. Because their leaves are tightly bound into a ball, they connote frugalness, holding on, and protecting your resources. Eat them when you're trying to save money or reduce expenses. Roast them with garlic and balsamic vinegar to banish a financial threat. Brussels sprouts grow in cool weather, which indicates their hardiness. Therefore, kitchen witches can also turn to them when doing spells for strength, endurance, and longevity. Rich in vitamins C and K, Brussels sprouts may even have the potential to help prevent cancer.

Folklore says Brussels sprouts grew from bitter tears. Nearly a thousand years ago, these cruciferous vegetables were cultivated near Brussels, Belgium (hence their name), where it was believed that eating them could prevent drunkenness.

Cabbage

One of the oldest cultivated vegetables, cabbage grows wild in a variety of colors, including white, red, and green. Despite its unpleasant smell, this cruciferous vegetable has long been linked with love. You can make a magic ink from purple cabbage, perfect for writing spells for love or money. Chop the cabbage into small pieces and simmer them in water until the water turns a deep reddish purple. Keep your intention in mind as you work. Strain out the chunks and cook the liquid until it's the consistency you want.

Dip an old-fashioned quill or fountain pen in your magic ink and write an affirmation, incantation, or other spell with it.

In medieval times, newlyweds ate cabbage soup to ensure a long, happy, and fertile marriage. Couples also planted cabbage in their gardens to bring good luck and prosperity. According to Celtic folklore, young women pulled up cabbages on Samhain to determine who they would marry—if a lot of soil clung to the cabbage's roots, the querent's spouse would be rich. The eighteenth-century Scottish poet Robert Burns mentioned this custom in his poem "Halloween."

Caraway

Kitchen witches know that the herb caraway helps protect you and your home from thieves as well as harmful or mischievous spirits. Use caraway in house-blessing spells by sprinkling some seeds in the corners of each room to chase away bad vibes. Put a few seeds in your purse. Fill a small cloth bag with seeds and place it in your jewelry box. Grow fresh caraway in a garden or a container beside the entrance to your home. According to folklore, caraway in an amulet placed in a cradle will keep evil entities from stealing a baby.

While caraway isn't normally thought of as an herb for love spells, you can use it to safeguard a relationship if you feel a partner's interest may be waning. Bake the seeds along with a bit of rosemary and dill in bread, then share it with your partner to encourage fidelity. You may want to give loaves of homemade bread to friends, too, for the seeds can strengthen any relationship.

In terms of cooking, caraway seeds give rye bread its characteristic flavor. They aid digestion and calm stomach problems too.

Carob

Called "the black gold of Cyprus," the ever-green carob tree grows mainly in the Middle East and Mediterranean regions. The word *carat* derives from *carob* because goldsmiths once used the seed pods to weigh gold. Because of these associations, kitchen witches can carry a whole seed pod or fashion talismans that include carob seeds to attract wealth. Bake carob brownies or carob-chip cookies and add macadamia nuts, which are also associated with prosperity. A dish of carob-mint-chip ice cream is a sweet way to encourage financial gain, for both mint and carob contain money-drawing qualities.

Caffeine-free carob powder is a natural sweetener and can take the place of cocoa in most baked goods that call for chocolate. Considered to be healthier than cocoa, it's higher in fiber and has long been used as a digestive aid. It's rich in antioxidants too. And unlike chocolate, carob isn't toxic to dogs and cats, so you needn't worry if your pet nibbles some.

Carrot

Viewed from the perspective of sympathetic magic, it's easy to see the connection between carrots and male fertility. The vegetable's obvious phallic shape symbolically links carrots with men and male energy as well as characteristics that have tra-ditionally been associated with the masculine/yang force, such as action, assertiveness, courage, and strength. For this reason, the ancient Greeks used carrots in love spells to stimulate male virility and desire. Contemporary kitchen witches can too. Want to spark passion and romance in a relationship? Bake a carrot cake and share it with your lover—the tasty dessert blends this sexy "masculine" vegetable with "feminine" cream cheese frosting (ruled by the Moon) and sugar (ruled by Venus).

Carrots and other root vegetables are among the oldest cultivated crops—the Babylonians grew them thousands of years ago. Our ancestors liked them because they're easy to grow, nutrient dense, and hardy and have a long shelf life. Carrots are also rich in the antioxidant beta carotene, which your body converts to vitamin A, a nutrient that supports good vision; this may be why carrots have long been linked with good health. If you're embarking on a vision quest or want to see what the future holds, eating carrots may help.

Cauliflower

Remember the old folktale that babies come from cabbage patches? Perhaps that story arose from the knowledge of cauliflower's magical connection with fertility, based on the vegetable's abundant florets. A head of cauliflower looks a bit like a brain, too, which may be the reason it's sometimes linked with intelligence. The ancient Egyptians ate it for mental clarity. Mark Twain called it "a cabbage with a college education." When you seek answers to a problem, try eating cauliflower to gain insight.

Although most people think of it in the popular white variety, cauliflower also comes in green, orange, and purple. Choose the color that corresponds to your intentions (see Chapter 4 for more information about color symbolism).

Because cauliflower is so versatile and modifiable, you can combine it with an array of spices, herbs, and other vegetables to produce the magical results you desire. Add ginger and curry powder to make an Indian dish with zing that will bring inspiration and new ideas. Bake it with cheese to encourage feelings of comfort, nurturance, and safety. Mix it with other vegetables that represent your intentions, such as spinach for strength, onions for protection, green bell peppers for prosperity, or sweet potatoes for groundedness.

Cayenne (Red Pepper)

Hot and spicy cayenne revs up spells. Added to meats, vegetables, soups, stews, sauces, and condiments, it speeds the action of a working and heightens the intensity. Ruled by Mars, the planet witches associate with sexuality, passion, vitality, motivation, and assertiveness, cayenne pepper sparks desire; therefore, it's a natural ingredient in spells to increase excitement in a romance or to renew a lover's ardor. If a relationship is slow to get off the ground, pull out the cayenne and let it work its magic.

Cayenne's stimulating nature can also nudge a condition that's gotten stuck. In addition to sprinkling cayenne on a meal, you can put dried peppers in a talisman. Use red pepper to add impetus to an important business deal that's languishing or to release money that's been owed to you. You can also ignite creativity and animate communication with cayenne, but go easy with this potent pepper, for too much may incite arguments and discord.

Cayenne peppers also have many health benefits—they contain vitamins C, A, B$_6$, and K. Their antioxidant properties can protect you against inflammation, and they may improve heart-related conditions, including high blood pressure.

Celery

Kitchen witches turn to celery to strengthen their psychic powers and intellectual clarity. Celery is ruled by Mercury, the planet astrologers associate with the mind and communication.

Eat celery seeds when you need to concentrate or focus on casting a spell. Munch them before taking a test, entering into a negotiation, or giving a speech. Celery can also help ease mental stress and clear away unwanted thoughts. Put the seeds in a charm bag and sleep with it under your pillow to bring prophetic dreams, or combine them with star anise to facilitate astral travel. Before meditation, you can eat celery to calm mental restlessness, open you up to spiritual guidance, and bring peace of mind.

Celery has long been celebrated in history. The Greek poet Homer discussed celery in his epic the *Odyssey* circa the late eighth century B.C.E. Confucius wrote about it, too, almost as long ago. The ancient Romans considered celery an aphrodisiac; the ancient Greeks crowned the winners of musical competitions with it; the ancient Egyptians placed it in King Tut's tomb. During the Victorian era, the elite displayed it in vases as centerpieces on their dinner tables, much in the same way you might display flowers today.

Chamomile

Witches love this pretty herb with its fragrant yellow flowers for its ability to soothe body, mind, and spirit. Its gentle action eases tension and anxiety and helps restore balance after an emotional upset or stressful event. Chamomile is a mainstay in the apothecaries of kitchen witches and herbalists. Place the dried herb in a talisman to attract peaceful circumstances or in an amulet to ward off bad vibes or animosity. The flowers can be added to candles, soaps, and lotions to enhance relaxation—the aromatherapy benefits also support meditation and invite guidance from spirit helpers.

Chamomile is best known as a nervine and a digestive aid. It soothes upset stomachs and quells nausea. A cup of chamomile tea before bedtime is a safe, natural tonic for insomnia. Put some in a sleep pillow to bring sweet dreams. Added to bathwater, the herb eases aches, pains, and stiffness while also softening the skin. Folklore tells that chamomile even has a positive effect on other plants; when grown in an herb garden, it supports the health and well-being of its neighbors. Although chamomile's medicinal and magical uses can be traced back to ancient Egypt, the English brought this plant to its current level of popularity.

Cheese

Cheese isn't something people usually think of as an oracle, but two thousand years ago a seer named Artemidorus wrote about a method of fortune-telling with cheese called "tyromancy." Ask a question, then cut a slice of Swiss cheese and count the holes. Look up the meaning of that number (according to numerology) to get your answer. During the

Middle Ages, people believed cheese had the psychic ability to identify thieves and murderers too. Celtic legends say fairies like cheese and they'll bring a good harvest if people give them this favorite food. If you do spellwork with the fae, offer them cheese to win their assistance. Eating cheese can help to manifest intentions. Carve runes or other symbols on a piece of cheese to represent what you desire—good health, prosperity, and so on—then eat it to make your wish come true. If you hope to win a person's love, carve *gifu*, the Norse rune for relationships (it looks like an *X*), or a heart on a piece of cheese and feed it to your intended.

Cheese has been said to possess other magical talents too. In the *Odyssey*, the Greek poet Homer wrote that the goddess Circe concocted a witch's brew made with cheese, wine, barley, and honey that turned men into animals. And the English medieval historian William of Malmesbury insisted that female innkeepers in Italy used cheese to change their customers into animals, though why remains a question.

Symbolically, cheese represents transformation, for when milk curdles, it becomes cheese. And because it's made of milk, from which all young mammals draw their first sustenance, it is associated with nourishment, comfort, fertility, and motherly love. Kitchen witches can boost the magical benefits of herbs, fruits, and other edibles by combining or pairing them with cheese—the cheese will nourish your objectives.

Cherry

Although popular Western slang connects *cherry* with virginity, in witchcraft, cherries signify the opposite. The cherry, with its single seed in the center of the fruit, resembles a fertile womb.

Therefore, according to symbolic magic, cherries have magical properties that can enhance fertility, whether that means children of the body or of the mind. The fruit's deep red color also symbolizes love, sexuality, passion, and desire. Bake a cherry pie and share it with a lover to inspire lust.

In Japan, the beautiful cherry trees that blossom each spring represent new beginnings, joy, and good fortune. At the Hanami festival, people come together under cherry trees to celebrate the joys of family, friends, and loved ones. A Buddhist story says the cherry tree gave support to the mother of the Buddha while she gave birth. Myths also tell that the cherry tree holds the secret to immortality.

The cherry tree's pretty reddish-brown wood is prized by furniture makers and carvers, but it also has magical properties, according to Celtic lore. Legends say drinking from a cup carved from a cherry tree's burl will bring good fortune. Sharing a cup of wine from a cherrywood quaich (a two-handled cup) with a lover ensures a long and happy relationship. Cherry is also a favorite wood for kitchen cabinets. If you're building or renovating your kitchen, you may want to consider cherry for its magical qualities as well as its aesthetic ones.

Chilis

Spicy hot chilis can intensify any magic working. When used in spells, they stimulate the actions of other ingredients. Add fresh chilis to soups, stews, casseroles, and other dishes to bring about quick results. Put dried chili peppers in talismans, amulets, and charm bags when your goal is to invigorate, enliven, or speed up a situation. In love spells, chili peppers spark passion. In spells for success, they boost confidence and daring. Athletes may want to add chili peppers to their diets to heighten their energy and sharpen their competitive edge.

Ruled by the planet Mars, chilis (fresh or dried) embody all the things associated with the element of fire: heat, assertiveness, competitiveness, vitality, and lust. The ancients burned peppers to ward off vampires, werewolves, and other bad creatures.

Chili peppers also have powerful antioxidant properties that can aid wound healing and immune function. They're also high in vitamins A, C, B_6, K_1, and potassium, and eating them may benefit your blood and bones.

Chives

Chives' sharp scent helps clear and focus the mind as well as improve memory and communication. In spells that involve affirmations or incantations, write your intention on a piece of paper, then put a pinch of dried chives on the paper, fold it, and tie it with ribbon in a color that corresponds to your objective (see Chapter 4 for a list of color correspondences). Tuck the paper in a notch in a tree and let it deteriorate naturally. Your spell will come to fruition when the paper has dissolved.

This member of the onion family shares its cousin's powers of protection. In the Middle Ages, chives were believed to break curses and guard against diseases as well as to end harmful habits and indulgences. Kitchen witches snip fresh chives on food not only for their flavor but also to repel unwanted energies. You can also crush chives between your fingertips, then rub the juice on candles or ritual tools to purify them in preparation for magical workings.

Easy to grow in a garden, window box, or container, fresh chives add a delectable flavor to meat, chicken, fish, and egg dishes as well as salads, soups, and vegetables.

Chocolate

For kitchen witches, chocolate—especially the rich, dark variety—is a key ingredient in love spells. Bake chocolate cakes, cookies, pies, or brownies and serve them to a partner to inspire affectionate feelings. You might want to decorate your confection with pink icing hearts too. During preparation, project loving thoughts into the batter. Or, share a banana split with hot fudge sauce and strawberries with a lover. (The banana has obvious phallic symbolism, and the bright red strawberries resemble the heart.)

The ancient Mayans believed chocolate had spiritual qualities. The Aztecs drank it as an aphrodisiac. Perhaps one reason for this is that chocolate contains tryptophan, which releases serotonin in the brain and makes you feel better. Chocolate also increases dopamine and affects the brain's pleasure center. So it's no surprise people associate chocolate with love. (Giving turnips on Valentine's Day doesn't have quite the same appeal, does it?)

Cinnamon

Ruled by Jupiter, the planet astrologers associate with growth and expansion, delicious cinnamon increases the power of magical workings. Witches prize it especially for its ability to enhance career success and attract wealth. Cinnamon also stimulates action and can help generate quick results. Want to jump-start your career? Try eating cinnamon buns or toast for breakfast. Sprinkle powdered cinnamon on your chai or latte if you're looking to get a raise. If your creativity is flagging or that promotion you've been expecting still hasn't come through, put a bowl of cinnamon sticks on your desk to stir things up. Cinnamon's magical power isn't limited to career matters, however. This favorite spice can broaden your mental and spiritual horizons as well.

Cinnamon hails from Southeast Asia, where its leaves, flowers, bark, and roots have played a role in traditional medicine for millennia. In ancient Egypt, the spice was so precious it was considered a gift fit for kings. Recent research in the West suggests the herb may aid in combating diabetes and might lower blood sugar as well as cholesterol. It's also an antioxidant that can protect against damage caused by free radicals.

Clove

Tangy cloves not only stimulate the taste buds, they also stimulate financial growth when used in spells. Kitchen witches add them to meat dishes, stews, and soups to invite prosperity and abundance of all kinds. When baking a ham, insert eight whole cloves (or a multiple of eight) into the meat—eight is the number of financial stability and material gain. Cloves are an important ingredient in gingerbread too. Magically, ginger speeds up a spell's action, so blending the two spices brings money your way more quickly.

Prepare a potpourri with cloves, cinnamon sticks, and orange peel and let it simmer on the stove. The fragrant mixture will fill your kitchen with a tantalizing aroma that attracts good fortune. (Cinnamon, as mentioned previously, encourages growth, and orange uplifts the spirits, so the three make a potent combination.) When you're on the go, suck a tasty candy clove ball or chew clove-flavored gum to remind you of your intention to attract wealth. Witches also use cloves to enhance psychic vision. Dress a candle with clove essential oil and burn it in your kitchen, or place the candle on your altar to open your inner sight.

Before modern dentistry, people tucked cloves inside their cheeks to soothe toothaches and gum problems. Clove's antibacterial properties can still support oral health—add the oil to toothpaste, or floss with clove-flavored dental floss. (One caveat: More isn't necessarily better, however, as overuse can irritate gums and skin inside your mouth.)

Coconut

Coconut's tough outer shell symbolizes protection. Cut a coconut in half and fill the interior with basil, oregano, garlic, and other protection herbs. Tie the nut back together again and bury it near your home to safeguard your loved ones and property. Charge the milk under the full moon and drink it to provide protection. You can use the shells as cups or bowls too. Scrape out the meat, then carve sigils on the inside and drink a magic potion or eat a magic meal from the coconut shell. You can burn the shells in a ritual fire for protection too.

Ancient Sanskrit texts say the coconut tree "provides all the necessities of life" and credit it with bringing wealth and good health. The nut's three "eyes" represent the past, present, and future. Associated with fertility, it's a popular offering in temples and at celebrations and is shared at wedding festivals for good fortune.

Coconuts are a good source of healthy fat as well as a number of minerals, including manganese, copper, and iron. They also contain antibacterial and antioxidant properties. Substitute coconut milk in recipes if you're lactose intolerant; use coconut flour instead of wheat if you want to go gluten-free.

Coffee

Coffee speeds up the action of a spell. Add coffee beans to a talisman to bring quick results. Grind coffee beans and smell the rich, fragrant aroma to help motivate you when you want to break out of a rut, remove an obstacle, or make a change. Would you like to see more action or excitement in some area of your life? Store coffee in the section of your kitchen that corresponds to that area (see the information about feng shui in Chapter 4).

Coffee helps you get going in the morning or gives you an energy boost when you need to stay up late to finish a rush project. Coffee clears the mind and sparks imagination, which is why it's a favorite of creative people. Kitchen witches can use it in spells for creative inspiration and can draw on coffee's stimulating properties in other ways too.

You can even scry with coffee. Brew a pot of French roast, let it cool, and pour some in a plain white bowl. Then gaze into the coffee as if it were a dark mirror, and let impressions arise in your mind.

Corn

Witches associate corn with prosperity, especially yellow corn because it is reminiscent of gold. Hang dried ears of corn on your front door to invite prosperity to your home. You can also add dried kernels to talisman bags to attract wealth. Bake corn bread and serve it with beans for good fortune—add jalapeños if you're in a hurry. Eat white corn to gain spiritual insight or to communicate with ancestors on the other side. Grind blue corn and scatter it outside your home for purification and protection. Fashion a poppet from corn husks and display it in your kitchen to bring happiness, good luck, and longevity.

For the Indigenous peoples of North and South America, corn has spiritual and magical associations. Hopi legends speak of corn maidens, deities who brought precious maize—the most important crop for many tribes—to nourish the people. The ancient Mayans revered a corn god who created humankind. Corn was more than a food source; it also symbolized wisdom and connected human beings to spirits and the divine realm.

Cranberry

Like other red fruits and vegetables, cranberries are associated with love, passion, vitality, self-confidence, courage, and enthusiasm. Although ruled by the planet Mars, the berries grow in watery bogs, so cranberries combine the elemental energies of both fire and water, masculine and feminine, action mixed with emotion. Therefore, cranberries are an ideal ingredient for love spells. Most people don't write spells in blood anymore, but if you feel a need to add extra color, use cranberry juice as your ink. In rituals, substitute cranberry juice for wine.

Harvested in late fall, cranberries find their way onto your plate between Samhain and Yule. In the US, Thanksgiving wouldn't be complete without cranberry sauce. Kitchen witches can make their own magical cranberry sauce and tweak it to suit their intentions. To counter the berries' tartness, blend in honey—honey will also enhance the sweetness in your relationships. Orange juice or zest increases happiness and optimism. Add cinnamon and/or cloves for career success and prosperity. Want to strengthen your psychic vision or communicate with spirits? Sprinkle in some nutmeg. Grate in a little ginger to speed up your spell.

Cranberries also offer many health benefits. They're powerful antioxidants with plenty of vitamin C to support your immune system. Natural healers recommend them for good urinary and kidney functioning too.

Cucumber

Astrologers assign rulership of cucumber to the Moon, giving it a feminine nature. From the perspective of sympathetic magic and symbolism, however, its phallic shape is definitely masculine. We're talking energy here, not gender, so there's no conflict. Cucumbers can relieve stress, promote harmony, and help establish balance in situations that have gotten out of whack.

Because cucumbers combine yin and yang, they're ideal for working any type of fertility magic. Folklore suggests putting a cucumber under your bed if you want to become pregnant. Artistic people can eat cucumbers to encourage creativity and strengthen connections with the muse. Add slices of refreshing cucumber to water and drink it to cool anger, irritation, impatience, or tension—or simply to chill on a hot summer day.

Prized for their hydrating properties, cucumbers can alleviate dry, chapped, or sunburned skin. Blend them into a lotion with aloe or other moisturizing ingredients to make a soothing face mask. Rub raw cucumbers on insect bites to ease itching. Lay cucumber slices on your eyes while you rest to soften wrinkles and reduce swelling.

Cumin

Draw upon cumin's energy to protect your property. Mix cumin with salt in a bowl and place the bowl near the entrance to your home or business to repel thieves. Or, sprinkle cumin seeds in a circle around your property. Carry a small pouch full of cumin in your purse to deter pickpockets. Make an amulet with cumin and stash it in the glove compartment of your car for safe journeys. And if you worry that your lover's heart might be stolen by another, make this spice a staple in your cooking. You can also add a pinch to wine and drink the magic brew to encourage fidelity.

Native to the Mediterranean region, cumin is a popular ingredient in Mexican and Indian cuisines. An herb of protection, cumin was used in earlier times to ward off evil spirits. The ancient Egyptians buried it with their dead to protect their spirits in the afterlife.

Used in traditional medicine, cumin can aid digestion and may help lower cholesterol. Some research suggests it may also be beneficial for dieters and diabetics.

Dill

Kitchen witches use dill to attract good luck, especially in financial matters. Combine the seeds with dried parsley and mint in a talisman to bring prosperity. Carry it with you to inspire confidence when you go for a job interview. In your workplace, dill can help dispel jealousy and unhealthy competition. Share it with colleagues to encourage cooperation. Fashion charms that include dill for your friends to promote congeniality. The herb's pleasing fragrance and gentle energy can also benefit love spells. Although it may not sound like a particularly romantic dish, potatoes (ruled by Venus, the planet of love and relationships) with a creamy dill sauce can generate positive feelings in a lover.

A tasty seasoning with vegetables, legumes, fish (especially salmon), seafood, and, of course, pickles, dill has a calming effect that encourages restful sleep and sweet dreams. It's easy to grow in a garden or a container on a kitchen windowsill. Hang a bunch of fresh dill above your bed or add dill seeds to a dream pillow to prevent nightmares and as a remedy for insomnia. Dill contains vitamins C and A and helps support the immune system. It's also a source of calcium, manganese, magnesium, and iron.

Egg

Because the egg itself looks like a pregnant womb, kitchen witches can use this symbolism in magic work. If you want to become pregnant, encourage creative endeavors, birth new projects, or nurture your inner child, incorporate eggs into your magic. Decorate eggs to represent your objectives. Color them with vegetable dyes that correspond to your intentions (see Chapter 4 for a list of color correspondences). Both the colors and the vegetables used to produce the colors you choose have magical symbolism. If you like, decorate the eggs with symbols that hold meaning for you.

According to mythology, a rabbit painted some eggs and delivered them as a gift to the Germanic goddess Ostare or Eostre, for whom the spring equinox sabbat Ostara is thought to be named. Ostare liked the pretty eggs so much she asked the rabbit to share them with the whole world. Our word for Easter derives from the goddess's name, and the custom of painting eggs at Easter has its roots in this myth.

The spring equinox is a time to celebrate life, renewal, rebirth, and creativity, when the earth awakens after her long winter's sleep. Flowers blossom, and baby animals and birds are born. Eggs, therefore, represent fertility (as do rabbits). Use a needle to poke holes in both ends of an egg, then blow out the insides and save the shell. Write magic words, symbols, or images on the shell, then set it on your altar—perhaps in a pretty eggcup—to "birth" an idea or intention and make it blossom.

Fennel

Witches value fennel for its numerous and varied magical properties, especially its ability to provide both physical and psychic protection. Like garlic, rowan, and basil, you can hang fennel above a doorway to keep unwanted intruders away from your home or workplace. Grow the plant on your kitchen windowsill to repel disruptive energies. Burn dried fennel and use the smoke to cleanse ritual tools. Our ancestors believed the herb conferred bravery on warriors, who drank fennel tea before going into battle. You can follow their lead to gain courage. Try chewing fennel seeds before confronting an adversary in the boardroom or on the playing field.

A relative of carrot and parsley, this popular ingredient in Mediterranean cuisine has been part of traditional medicine for millennia. The ancient Chinese considered it an antidote for snake bites; the ancient Greeks used it as an insect repellent. Fennel has long been considered a boon to eyesight due to its vitamin A content. (More than two thousand years ago, the Roman philosopher Pliny the Elder wrote that snakes ate it to sharpen their vision.) It also has anti-inflammatory and antibacterial properties. Fennel is also one of the main ingredients in absinthe.

Fig

Because the fig's shape reminds one of a woman's body, it's an obvious choice for fertility magic as well as for women's health issues that involve the reproductive system. Kitchen witches can also draw upon the fig's creative powers to support artistic endeavors. Eat them for inspiration or to help you earn money from your creative pursuits. Figs can benefit love spells too. Dry the seeds and include them in a talisman to attract a new partner or to strengthen an existing relationship.

In a number of cultures and mythologies, figs have spiritual associations. The Buddha is said to have gained enlightenment while meditating beneath a fig tree. According to some sources, the fruit of knowledge Adam and Eve ate was actually a fig, not an apple. Hindus connect the fig tree's roots with the god Brahma, the trunk with Vishnu, and the leaves with Shiva. This sacred fruit can assist you with your own spiritual growth and open your heart to receive divine love and guidance.

Garlic

Garlic's stimulating action makes it a good herb to use in spells you want to materialize quickly. Add garlic powder to talismans for career success or financial gain. Ruled by Mars, the planet astrologers associate with men, sex, assertiveness, and vitality, garlic can motivate a hesitant partner's interest or increase the excitement in a relationship. It also boasts a number of health benefits, including cleansing the blood.

You've no doubt heard stories about garlic's ability to keep vampires at bay, and perhaps its protective power is due to its strong odor. For thousands of years, people have hung chains of garlic bulbs above the doors to their homes or worn garlic around their necks to ward off all sorts of evil. Garlic also gets credit for providing safety from curses and other forms of malice and mayhem. Wearing a garlic necklace may be effective, but it's also stinky. Kitchen witches can find many other more agreeable ways to tap the power—and flavor—of this popular allium. Garlic plays a role in Mediterranean cuisine, Asian dishes, Mexican and South American cooking—just about every culture relies on this inexpensive and readily available ingredient to add a bit of zing.

Ginger

Kitchen witches tap ginger's sharp, tangy nature to speed up the action and intensity of spells. Consequently, you can combine it with other ingredients to boost their quickness and power. You can eat it or brew it in tea, add dried ginger-root or powder to charms, or rub the oil on crystals or gemstones used in spellcraft. In love potions or talismans, it stimulates excitement, emotions, and sexual desire. It can also spark mental activity, improve memory and learning skills, and aid communication—however, too much may encourage arguments.

This ancient rhizome hails from Southeast Asia and is valued around the world for its healing properties as well as its distinctive flavor—it's a staple in Chinese, Japanese, Indian, and Thai cooking. Its essential oil gingerol and natural antioxidant properties are responsible for many of ginger's healing benefits. One of the best plants for countering nausea and digestive complaints, ginger can soothe morning sickness, ease queasiness due to side effects of medications, relieve dyspepsia, stimulate appetite, reduce inflammation, and help the body assimilate nutrients from food. In aromatherapy, ginger's lively action counters sadness, fatigue, depression, apathy, and lack of motivation.

Grape

Historically, wine has been associated with fine dining, sophistication, and wealth. So the next time you're designing a prosperity spell or ritual, consider including wine or grapes in it. You may even want to sip a glass of vino while performing a prosperity spell, or share wine in your chalice during a ritual. Mabon celebrations, in particular, are good times to work spells with grapes because they occur during the season when the ripe fruit is harvested. Placing a cluster of plump, juicy grapes on your altar at the fall equinox represents fruitfulness, fertility, and Mother Earth's richness.

Wine is often linked with transformation. Remember the biblical story of Jesus changing water into wine? Fermentation is an act of transforming one substance (grapes, in this case) into something of a different nature (wine). If you want to transform something in your life, consider bringing grapes or wine into a spell or ritual.

Grapes possess healing properties too. They contain the antioxidants lutein and zeaxanthin, which can aid your eyes by protecting the retinas and preventing cataracts. Grapeseed oil is also a lovely carrier base for essential oils and is used in lotions for skin care, massage, and more.

Grapefruit

Like other citrus fruits, grapefruit's fresh, clean, tangy scent stimulates your awareness and sharpens mental clarity. Add a few drops of grapefruit essential oil to bathwater before performing a ritual, rite, or spell to cleanse the body, mind, and spirit. You can also mix a little grapefruit juice or a few drops of grapefruit essential oil in water, then spritz the mixture in a space you wish to purify for a ritual. Mist it in your home or workplace to eliminate unwanted energies and tension, especially after an argument or emotional upset.

Grapefruit's purifying properties can help you shed old, outdated ideas and behaviors. By clearing away past limitations, this fruit makes room for new opportunities and growth. Eating it can help you see confusing situations more clearly and come up with ways to deal with problems. Grapefruit can also encourage you to do some soul-searching and look more deeply into areas you may have been avoiding.

Eat grapefruit at breakfast to clear your mind, spark creativity, and awaken you to the day's possibilities. (Note: Grapefruit can interact unfavorably with some medications, so be sure to check for adverse reactions before including it in your diet.)

Green Bell Pepper

According to folklore, you can use green peppers in an unusual way for love spells. Cut a pepper in half and remove the seeds. Place photos of yourself and your partner inside the pepper, then tie or tape it shut. The pepper's womb-like shape nurtures your relationship. Peppers also contain protective qualities. Hang them to dry in your kitchen, where they can help prevent accidents and mishaps. Perhaps you've heard that peppers with three lobes are sweeter than the ones with four. From the perspective of numerology, however, three represents creativity whereas four correlates with stability and permanence, so the number of lobes could be a factor when you're using bell peppers in spellwork.

Like other green foods, sweet green bell peppers can be eaten to attract prosperity. Bell peppers come in yellow, orange, red, and purple too, and the color will indicate the type of spell for which it's appropriate. Combine them with other greens in salads or in Thai, Chinese, or Creole dishes. Bell peppers offer health benefits too; they're high in vitamin C and fiber and low in calories.

Honey

As you might expect, honey is a popular ingredient in love spells, for it brings sweetness to any relationship. Its stickiness can also help hold partners together during challenging times. You can include honey instead of sugar in many dishes that call for sweetener. Stir honey into tea or coffee (clockwise for attraction or increase). Eat treats such as baklava, challah, or sticky buns rich with honey to help you feel more loving. Honey goes well with salmon, chicken, and meatballs too. You can even dress candles with honey. Fairies are fond of honey, so you may want to leave it as an offering if you work magic with the fae.

According to Greek mythology, honey was a favorite food of Aphrodite, the goddess of love and beauty. Make a honey facial scrub to enhance your own beauty, or add it to bathwater as a prelude to romance. Hindu texts list honey as one of the five sacred elixirs of immortality. The ancient Egyptians used honey in their embalming rituals. Archaeologists have found honey in millennia-old tombs, and it's still edible, a testament to its properties of endurance and longevity. The Egyptians also applied honey to wounds to promote healing, a practice modern medicine has found to be effective as well.

Lavender

Witches incorporate lavender into love spells—the herb has a history of seduction that includes such notable temptresses as Cleopatra and the Queen of Sheba. Consider feeding candied lavender to a lover or decorating a cake with fresh lavender flowers. Blend lavender essential oil with a carrier oil (olive, jojoba, grapeseed) to create a sensuous massage lotion.

Lavender is also used for relaxation. Its aromatic properties deepen meditation and trance states. Its purifying scent can cleanse a sacred space in preparation for a ritual or other magic working. Hang bunches of fresh lavender in the corners of your home to protect against disruptive energies. Sprinkle your bed linens with lavender water to prevent nightmares and induce restful sleep. Stuff a healing pillow with rice and dried lavender, then heat it in the microwave to bring soothing warmth to aching joints and muscles. The plant is easy to grow in sunny, dry climes and, if you have the space, would be a welcome addition to any kitchen witch's garden.

For more than twenty-five hundred years, people have recognized lavender's powers of protection and preservation. The ancient Egyptians used it in mummification. Biblical passages refer to anointing Jesus' feet with lavender (or spikenard, as it was called then). Our ancestors stored clothing and linens in it and laid out their dead in lavender. In the days when people didn't wash as frequently as they do now, those who could afford it added lavender to their bathwater and laundry—they even scattered the herb on church floors to ward off evil spirits. Today, we know lavender has antibacterial and antifungal properties that helped produce the desired results.

Lemon

Lemon's crisp, clean scent makes it a natural for cleansing and purification spells. After an argument or upsetting experience, spritz your home with a blend of lemon juice and water to clear the air. Squeeze the juice of a lemon into bathwater to wash away old memories, attachments, and attitudes. Asperge participants with lemon water before a ritual. Purify ritual tools with lemon essential oil diluted in a carrier oil such as olive or grapeseed. Dress candles with it to clear the mind, stimulate mental activity, and make you more alert. Dot a handkerchief with lemon essential oil and sniff it before taking an exam or discussing an intellectually challenging topic with colleagues.

Mythology tells that lemons were so highly valued by the ancients that the fruit was included in the dowry of the Greek goddess Hera, wife of Zeus. Cultivated in Egypt for nearly three thousand years, lemons traveled with Columbus to the Americas, where they thrived in the Caribbean and Florida. The fruit became a staple aboard ships after a British physician in the mid-eighteenth century discovered it could prevent scurvy. Today, lemons and other citrus fruits are still prized as powerful antioxidants, rich in flavonoids and key sources of vitamin C.

Lettuce

When you're making salads, consider the characteristics of the lettuces you choose and combine them
to reflect your intentions. All green lettuces are linked
with prosperity spells—lettuce is even a slang term that
means money. Red leaf, because of the color red's connection with passion,
is a good choice for love magic. Soft, creamy butter lettuce encourages
peace, gentleness, and congeniality in relationships.

Contemporary kitchen witches might find it a stretch to see lettuce as
an aphrodisiac, but to the ancient Egyptians, lettuce represented sexuality.
The Romans, too, thought it increased male potency. Greek myths, however, present a darker view. Adonis, lover of the goddess Aphrodite, was
killed by a wild boar in a lettuce bed, which led to a connection between
this leafy vegetable and death.

Lime

Like lemons and other citrus fruits, limes play a role in
cleansing, clearing, and purification spells. Magically, you
can use limes in many of the same ways you use lemons. Mix
the juice in water and spritz a space to cleanse it before enacting a ritual.
Add it to bathwater to wash away any unwanted issues and concerns and
to stimulate your mental faculties. Lime, however, has a more lighthearted
and cheerful energy than lemon. Consequently, it can inspire happiness
and optimism. Our ancestors used limes to bless newly married couples
by chasing away negativity and to protect babies from evil spirits. Drink

water with lime in it to dispel your own inner demons and to free yourself from old attachments or habits that may be interfering with your current goals and aspirations.

Native to Southeast Asia, limes traveled on Spanish ships to the Caribbean, where they gained the names *key limes* and *Mexican limes*. In Malaysia, where limes grew natively, they were believed to protect against demons that caused disease (most likely because they're high in vitamin C).

Mango

Mangoes have come to represent sensuality, perhaps because of their lush sweetness. This connection, along with their traditional association with happiness, makes them a good choice for love spells. Like the peach, nectarine, and cherry, the mango is a stone fruit, meaning it holds a single hard seed inside, which symbolizes a pregnant womb. Therefore, you can use it in fertility magic. Carve the Norse rune *inguz* on the seed and carry it with you to encourage mental or physical creativity.

Used in Hindu spiritual rituals, mangoes have signified happiness and prosperity. It was a favorite fruit of the Mughal emperors, who considered it a divine fruit. The Buddha is said to have meditated beneath a mango tree. Even today, Hindus hang mango leaves near the entrances to their homes to prevent negativity from coming inside. Kitchen witches, regardless of culture or religious belief, can tap the powers of mangoes by preparing and enjoying popular Indian dishes such as chutneys, curries, dals, and pickles.

Marjoram

You can use this herb to bless a union or to attract a congenial mate. In love spells, marjoram invites happiness and encourages cooperation between partners. Business partners and coworkers can benefit from marjoram's energy too. If you're trying to come to an agreement, give each member of the team a small envelope filled with dried marjoram to bring to the negotiating table. After an argument, burn dried marjoram to clear the air. If you're going through a life change, especially one that's love related, dress a candle with marjoram oil and burn it for emotional support and good luck.

Similar to oregano, but with a somewhat sweeter flavor, marjoram is a nice spice to put in sauces and marinades for fish, chicken, and veal. It's easy to grow in a garden, window box, or container in your kitchen. Traditionally, marjoram tea has been used to treat the common cold and as an aid to digestion. The oil is also added to soaps and cosmetics.

Melon

Melons are associated with female fertility because their shape is reminiscent of a womb. Because orange is the color that corresponds to the second chakra and creativity, cantaloupes may be the best choice for fertility spells. Cantaloupes and muskmelons can also nurture and encourage artistic ability and productivity. You can eat bright red watermelons to encourage passion and heighten a woman's libido. Pale green honeydew melons can aid women's health and ease discomfort associated with menstruation.

Share the fruit with a partner to increase sweetness between you or to cool tempers after an argument. Sprinkle the melon with black pepper to add spice to a relationship. Dry the seeds and add them to a witch bottle or charm bag to bring love, peace, and joy into your life.

Milk

The first food humans and other mammals eat is milk. It's not surprising, therefore, that milk is associated with nourishment, motherly love, and life itself. This quintessential "comfort food" is an apt symbol for feminine energy and power.

June's full moon is sometimes referred to as the Honey Moon. This is a good time to make "moon milk." Mix honey and cinnamon into milk and share it with friends at full moon esbats. If you like, blend fruit such as strawberries, bananas, or peaches into the milky brew to attract or strengthen love relationships. Serve it warm and sip it for relaxation before bed. The phrase *milk and honey* suggests abundance too. Drink this magical beverage to attract good fortune and prosperity. Or make a delicious creamy custard that uses these ingredients and share the dessert with loved ones. Fairies are fond of milk and honey too, so if you work with the fae, offer them this treat to stay on their good side.

In mythology, the Egyptian goddess Isis, who personifies the Divine Mother, is often depicted nursing her son Horus. Also known as the Cow Goddess, she wears a headdress that combines two of her symbols: a cow's horns and a disc that represents the full moon. When Isis's husband Osiris was killed, Isis poured milk on his tomb to bring him back to life.

Mushroom

When you hear the term *magic mushrooms*, you probably think of psilocybin and other fungi that produce hallucinogenic effects. Indeed, mushrooms have aided sorcerers, shamans, and witches for centuries by expanding consciousness for journeying, trance work, and healing magic.

Even nonpsychotropic mushrooms contain magic properties that a kitchen witch can use in spellcraft. Ruled by Pluto, the planet astrologers connect with transformation, mushrooms can help you through an important growth experience or major life change. They can also open doors to the psychic realm, strengthen your intuition, and connect you with spirit guides. Because some mushrooms grow on rotten wood or cattle dung, they're linked with life, death, and rebirth—areas that fall into Pluto's realm. Consequently, you can eat mushrooms to give you courage and protection when you want to let go of old, limiting behaviors, habits, or attitudes.

If you do fairy magic, you may be familiar with "fairy rings," peculiar circles of mushrooms that appear overnight and are believed to be the result of fairies dancing. Legends warn that if you step inside a ring, you'll disappear into the land of the fae.

Mustard

Ruled by Mars, the planet astrologers associate with vitality, assertiveness, courage, and sex, spicy mustard adds zing to any magical working. In love spells, it stimulates passion and excitement in a romance that's grown a bit dull. It can

also help you capture the attention of a disinterested partner. In money magic, mustard can break open stagnant financial situations or help you get some quick cash when you need it. Draw a good luck sigil on a sandwich with this condiment to speed results. In spells for career success, mustard lets you stand out from the crowd and brings recognition. Put some powdered mustard in a talisman to help you beat out opponents for a job or promotion.

Mustard enhances vitality and gives athletes a competitive edge. Eat mustard when you feel a need for more courage or self-confidence—on the playing field or in the boardroom—or to boost your physical energy, especially after an illness. Our ancestors relied on this plant's fiery nature in mustard plasters to treat colds, flus, congestion, coughs, and muscle aches—and there's evidence to suggest they still have a place in herbal healing.

Nutmeg

Native to Indonesia, nutmeg was once so precious that the Dutch traded their interest in Manhattan for a nutmeg-producing island controlled by the British. Today, kitchen witches associate the spice with financial gain and prosperity in general. In addition to cooking with it, you can put whole nutmegs in talismans to attract wealth or success in a business venture. Carry a nutmeg in your pocket or purse to win money in a contest or game of chance. Grate a little into olive oil and dress candles with it to bring good luck, especially in financial matters.

An important ingredient in baked goods, nutmeg's magical properties include sharpening psychic vision and helping the kitchen witch connect with spirit beings. Therefore, you may want to whip up a batch of maple sugar cookies spiced with nutmeg for your next Samhain ritual. Toss powdered nutmeg in a Yule fire for good luck or sprinkle some on a cup of eggnog and sip it while doing a tarot reading to see what the New Year will bring. Herbal healers also consider nutmeg to be a natural antidepressant and mood elevator as well as an antioxidant that can help you age gracefully.

Nuts

Nuts are the seeds of the trees from which they grow. Therefore, they symbolize potential, fertility, rebirth, and continuity. Because the edible part of the nut is contained within a hard outer shell, nuts also represent protection.

Each type of nut holds its own unique properties that the kitchen witch can use in spellcraft. Hazelnuts, considered sacred to the Greek god Hermes, strengthen psychic vision. Eat them before doing a tarot reading or other type of divination. Walnuts and pecans support intellectual endeavors of all kinds because their wrinkled lobes resemble the human brain. Cashews' sweet flavor makes them a favorite in love spells. Macadamia nuts encourage abundance. Peanuts, which develop underground, bring stability and grounding, especially in financial and business matters.

Combine nuts with other foods to produce the magical results you desire. Pecan pie's sweet, rich flavor aids cooperation and communication in romantic partnerships. Eat cookies made with walnuts and chocolate to spark creativity and imagination. Peanut butter helps protect your investments and promotes slow, steady growth in financial areas. Eat pistachio ice cream for comfort and protection, especially in family relationships.

Oat

Native to Europe, Asia, and northern Africa, oats are linked with comfort, nurturing, security, family, fertility, and tradition. In the days when our ancestors built bonfires at Beltane (May 1) and drove their livestock between the fires to ensure fertility, people threw oat cakes into the flames as offerings to the deities. Modern-day witches can eat oat cakes on this sabbat or toss them into a cook fire to encourage fertility in body or mind.

Alone, oats taste a bit bland, but they combine well with fruit, nuts, and other foods. Choose additional ingredients according to your intentions. If your objective is to sweeten family relationships, bake oatmeal chocolate chip cookies with brown sugar. Oatmeal granola topped with fresh bananas or strawberries can help bring stability to a romantic relationship. Add coconut milk if you hope to become pregnant. Fruit-and-nut bars are another good way to blend the characteristics of oats with other objectives. Walnuts and pecans aid mental pursuits; hazelnuts strengthen intuition; raisins (dried grapes) aid prosperity.

Olive/Olive Oil

Not only is olive oil healthier and tastier than seed oils, it contains qualities that kitchen witches can use to attract peace, strength, and prosperity. Witches also connect olives with longevity because the trees can live more than a thousand years.

Consider the type of olive when deciding which of the many varieties best suits your purposes. They come in green, gold, purple, and black, and each color has its own properties. Generally speaking, the darker the fruit, the riper it is. Kalamatas are considered the king of olives in Greek dishes, and perhaps it's no coincidence that they're purple, the color of royalty. Use them in spells for success, leadership, and personal power. Because of their large size and greenish-gold color, Cerignola olives are a good choice for prosperity spells.

Mythology tells us the goddess Athena gave the olive tree to Greece, where it has been a major source of nourishment and wealth for millennia. Other legends describe heroes using olive branches as weapons to slay ferocious beasts. In the biblical story of the great flood, a dove returns to Noah's ark holding an olive branch to signify that the storm has ended and peace on earth is restored. The Great Seal of the United States features an eagle holding an olive branch in one talon and arrows in the other, signifying the power of peace and war.

Onion

Like garlic, onions have been used for centuries to ward off evil spirits and unwanted intruders—their odor may have had something to do with this. The ancient Egyptians believed onions absorbed harmful energies. If you want to get rid of negativity, cut a raw onion into quarters and leave a piece in each corner of your kitchen overnight. In the morning, bury the onion a distance from your home. Plant onions in your garden or in containers to protect your home. Ruled by Mars, the planet astrologers connect with vitality, courage, war, and competition, onions can boost your energy and confidence when you're facing challenges.

Long ago, people used a form of divination with onions, called "crom-niomancy," to learn how loved ones who lived far away were faring. The querent carved the name of a friend or relative on an onion, then waited for it to sprout. If it sprouted quickly, all was well. Onions also helped people make a choice between two options, and kitchen witches can use this tactic as well. Here's how it works: Write one option on each of two onions; the one that sprouts first is what you should go with. Peeling away the layers of an onion represents removing blockages to uncover secrets and get to the truth of a matter. Try doing this to gain insight into a situation or to connect with your inner wisdom.

Orange

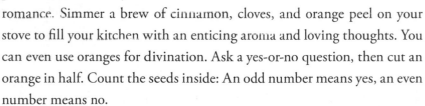

Like many fruits, oranges have magical associations with love and fertility. Put dried orange peel in a love talisman or include it in pot-pourri and set it in your bedroom to attract romance. Simmer a brew of cinnamon, cloves, and orange peel on your stove to fill your kitchen with an enticing aroma and loving thoughts. You can even use oranges for divination. Ask a yes-or-no question, then cut an orange in half. Count the seeds inside: An odd number means yes, an even number means no.

Not only are oranges rich in vitamin C to protect against colds, the essential oil lifts your spirits and can be a tonic for stress, anxiety, and insomnia. Dab some on your wrist or a handkerchief and sniff it to elevate your mood. Kitchen witches connect sweet oranges with joy and opti-mism. Begin your day with a glass of fresh-squeezed orange juice while you set an intention to enjoy good health and happiness.

Native to China and Southeast Asia, oranges first traveled to Europe along the Silk Road and were then spread far and wide by Portuguese seafarers. Today, oranges are the most popular fruits in the world. But before the days of widespread refrigeration, oranges were rare and expensive treats, presented proudly as gifts at Christmas.

Oregano

Oregano has always had a reputation as a potent good luck herb that inspires love, happiness, friendship, family togetherness, and abundance. Plant it in a garden in a sunny spot or in a container in your kitchen so you always have the fresh herb on hand. Include dried oregano in a love charm to strengthen romantic feelings and ensure fidelity—the herb is ruled by Venus, the planet of love and relationships. You can put a live plant in your bedroom to spice up your sex life. If a loved one passes from the earth realm, folklore recommends that you burn oregano or plant it on the person's grave to help you let go of sadness and resolve attachment.

Like its cousin basil, oregano also offers protection, especially in the home. Put pinches of the dried herb in the corners of each room to safeguard your property and your loved ones. Position a plant near the entrance to your home to ward off unwanted entities. Oregano can also help clear the air after an argument or emotional upset, dispel tensions, and restore balance and harmony. Oregano not only gives flavor to your favorite tomato, vegetable, and meat dishes, its uplifting energy also makes mealtime more congenial.

Paprika

This bright red herb has a flavor that's sweet, smoky, and spicy all at the same time. It's ruled by the planet Mars, which revs up the action and power of spells. Therefore, you can use paprika in your magical workings to speed results when time is of the essence. Its energy isn't quite as stimulating or aggressive as cayenne—although the hotter varieties can rival red pepper's action—and it includes a subtle sweetness that makes it perfect for love spells. Put powdered paprika in charms to spark new love or to heighten passion in an existing romantic relationship.

An easy way to tap paprika's energy is to dust it on deviled eggs to encourage fertility. Eggs, of course, represent creativity of the mind as well as the body, and paprika sparks enthusiasm in every way. The spice can inspire imagination and originality in artistic or inventive endeavors. It also boosts your energy so you can embark on a new venture or project, confident that you'll succeed. Use paprika in spells to beat out the competition too, on the playing field or in the boardroom.

Parsley

Witches link parsley with prosperity, especially in the US, where healthy green herbs bring to mind the green paper money of that country. Whenever you add parsley to a dish you're preparing, focus your intention on attracting abundance. Include dried parsley in prosperity talismans. Put a coin in a flowerpot to represent your intention, then plant parsley seeds in the pot; whenever you water it, think or say an affirmation to attract wealth.

Like its relative cilantro, parsley's healing properties date back to antiquity. Herbalists use its leaves, seeds, oil, and roots for medicinal purposes. An antioxidant high in vitamin K, an important vitamin for blood clotting, it's said to be beneficial in preventing and treating all sorts of blood-related conditions, including high blood pressure and blood sugar imbalances.

In terms of cooking, parsley is a favorite in soups, stews, sauces, and salads—and its crisp, clean flavor helps to freshen the breath. Parsley is also easy to grow—you might want to plant some in your garden or in a pot in your kitchen so you'll always have the fresh herb available.

Pea

Kitchen witches connect peas with abundance, due to their green coloring, and fertility, because a pod contains numerous individual peas, like a mother with many children. The next time you shell peas, notice how many are in a pod—the number could hold significance (see the section on numerology in Chapter 4). Eating peas can be a way to encourage prosperity. Put dried peas in talismans to attract good fortune and luck. If you have a garden, plant peas early in the spring to spark new opportunities.

Nobody is quite sure where the pea originated—archaeologists say we've been eating them for ten thousand years. In earlier times, peas were dried so they could be stored for long periods and made into soups, stews, or pottages such as the "pease porridge" of nursery rhyme fame. Sometimes, mint was added for flavor, although long-ago kitchen witches may have known the connection between mint and prosperity and included it for good luck in this peasant's dish. During the Renaissance, sweet garden peas eaten fresh became a favorite of the aristocracy.

Peach

Peaches are associated with love, peace, and harmony. And because this stone fruit with its single inner seed resembles a pregnant womb, it represents fertility. Wear a peach pit on a cord around your neck if you want to get pregnant, or to increase love and affection in a romantic relationship. Make a peach pie or cobbler and share it with a partner to bring joy. The peach tree's beautiful pink blossoms, which appear in the spring, symbolize womanhood. Traditionally, newly engaged Chinese women display peach blossoms in their homes to attract happiness and good luck in marriage.

In Asian cultures, the peach is also considered to bring longevity, even immortality. According to Chinese mythology, the goddess Wangmu Niangniang lives atop Mount Kunlun, where a rare peach tree grows in her garden. The tree puts forth fruit only once every three thousand years, and anyone who eats the goddess's magic peaches becomes immortal.

Pear

The pear symbolizes female fertility and power because of its curvy, feminine shape. Kitchen witches can use pears magically in the same ways as peaches, although pear energy is a little lighter and gentler. Spells for fertility, love, and romance can benefit from the inclusion of pears. Put pear seeds in a talisman to attract a lover. Wear pear essential oil as an aphrodisiac, or add it to water and spritz your bedroom with it. Place a vase of pretty white pear blossoms on your altar or in the relationships gua of your kitchen (see the section on feng shui in Chapter 4) to bring love and affection.

Pears have been prized for thousands of years. In his epic the *Odyssey*, the Greek poet Homer called the pear a gift from the gods. Mythology tells that pears were sacred to the Greek goddesses Hera, Aphrodite, and Athena as well as the Egyptian goddess Isis. In Chinese culture, pears are associated with wisdom, justice, and longevity. Other Asian cultures connect the fruit with good fortune and protection. The Emperor Charlemagne grew them in his gardens in the late eighth and early ninth centuries and during the medieval period, European monks excelled at cultivating pears. Today, there are about three thousand varieties of pears to enjoy.

Peppermint

Like all the mint varieties, peppermint is a favorite prosperity herb in witchcraft. A hardy and prolific plant, it represents wealth and can benefit most money spells. Dress candles with peppermint essential oil and burn them when you want to attract money and other material goodies. In candy, ice cream, confectionary, and other treats, peppermint is reminiscent of the sweetness of life and, as such, brings blessings to kitchen witches and their loved ones.

Peppermint's refreshing, purifying qualities make it ideal for cleansing rituals and in spells for renewal. After experiencing trauma, grief, or loss, let peppermint infuse your perspective with hope and healing. It helps you release old sorrows, clears outdated and limiting thinking and behavior patterns, and shows you a fresh, new direction in life, one that will bring abundance in many forms. In some cases, peppermint can inspire psychic insights or communication with spirits.

A noted digestive herb, peppermint soothes stomach upsets, nausea, heartburn, and other related complaints. It blends well with ginger and chamomile in tea to counteract adverse reactions to medications or in detoxing. Peppermint's cleansing properties make it an ideal ingredient in toothpaste, mouthwash, soap, and skincare products that relieve eczema, psoriasis, and other irritations.

Persimmon

Fall-ripening persimmons can be used to predict the weather, according to folklore. Cut one open vertically from the top to the bottom and examine the seeds, which are shaped like cutlery. A fork-shaped seed indicates a mild winter; one that looks like a knife suggests sharp, bitter winds; a seed in the shape of a spoon, which represents a shovel, means you'll get a lot of snow in the coming months.

The persimmon tree's wood is among the hardest and has been used to make golf clubs and pool cues. You might want to consider it for your magic wand. Burn the wood in a ritual fire for protection, strength, or endurance. Early Americans brewed persimmon beer and wine, as well as roasting and grinding the seeds to make a substitute for coffee. You can make healthy teas with them too—the fruit contains antioxidants, flavonoids, and tannins that can be beneficial for the heart and blood pressure. Persimmons are also high in vitamins A and C.

Pineapple

Pineapples have long been connected with prosperity, friendship, and good luck. Its many scales bring to mind armor, suggesting the fruit's powers of protection. Want to protect your assets or secure your financial picture? Encourage cooperation and congenial business relationships? Bake a pineapple upside-down cake and share it with colleagues to sweeten a deal. Pineapple can also help you attract friends or improve relationships with neighbors.

In some coastal cities of the eastern US, pineapples symbolize hospitality. In port cities during the eighteenth century, sea captains, sailors, and merchants traditionally displayed pineapples to indicate the safe return of their ships and to welcome neighbors in celebration. Columbus is credited with having brought pineapples to Europe from South America. Because it grew in tropical climes, rich Europeans and others in colder regions paid dearly for this rare fruit until the seventeenth century, when people in the northern hemisphere started growing it.

Healthwise, pineapple aids digestion by helping your body break down proteins. Plus, it's high in vitamin C to boost immune function and has anti-inflammatory properties. Drink pineapple juice after a workout to ease muscle soreness.

Plum

Myths say the divinities ate plums for good health and vitality. Kitchen witches, too, can eat them to encourage well-being and good fortune. The fruit's deep purple color is reminiscent of the royal purple only rulers were once allowed to wear, thus it symbolizes esteem and leadership. Today, the term *plum* means something great, wonderful, or choice, such as a plum job. Remove the plum's seed and carve the rune *berkana* (growth), *jera* (harvest), or *fehu* (fulfillment) on it. Wear it on a cord around your neck or carry it in a charm bag to attract the success you desire. Purple is also the color of the crown chakra, which connects you with the Divine. Fashion a staff made of plum wood to bring honor, wisdom, and power—spiritual as well as physical.

In Chinese culture, the beautiful plum tree with its delicate pink flowers symbolizes spring, hope, and the promise of good things to come after winter's barrenness. Put a vase of fragrant plum blossoms in your kitchen or on your dining table to welcome opportunities and celebrate new beginnings. Eating plums can help you through a transition from hard times to better days.

Pomegranate

Kitchen witches link pomegranates with life, death, and transitions of all kinds. If you're going through a personal transition, eating pomegranates can help you gain insight into the changes you're experiencing and make the best of them. The fruit can be used in magic for transformation too, such as ending an unhealthy relationship or kicking a bad habit. Because pomegranates have so many seeds contained in a womb-like shape, they also represent fertility and abundance. If you want to become pregnant, use pomegranates in your magical workings. You can also add the dried seeds to a talisman for prosperity. The fruit's deep red color is reminiscent of blood, so you can substitute the juice for blood in a spell if you don't feel like opening a vein.

The most famous myth about pomegranates is the story of the Greek goddess Demeter and her daughter Persephone. One day while out picking flowers, Persephone is kidnapped by the god Hades and held captive in the underworld. While imprisoned, the girl eats some pomegranate seeds, which ensures she'll never see her home again. However, the deities eventually work out a deal that allows Persephone to return to earth during the warm months. The myth, of course, symbolizes the changing of seasons.

Potato

The potato comes in five thousand varieties, in a wide array of colors, sizes, and shapes. Kitchen witches can draw upon those different colors and shapes for all sorts of magic. Purple potatoes support a union of earthly and spiritual power. Heart-shaped potatoes may be part of a love spell. (See Chapter 4 for more information about the symbolism of colors and shapes.) The potato's hardiness can be an asset in spells for strength, endurance, and permanence. Because potatoes combine well with meat, fish, and other vegetables, you can concoct magic soups, stews, and casseroles with them that express and support your intentions.

Native to Peru, potatoes have been raised for thousands of years. The Inca even honored a potato goddess named Axomama, who was one of the daughters of the earth mother goddess Pachamama. The Spanish brought potatoes to Europe during the Renaissance, where they became a staple in people's diets. However, the potato didn't gain instant favor there. To encourage farmers to grow them, the French king Louis XVI wore potato flowers in his buttonhole, and Marie Antoinette decorated her hair with the blossoms. When famine struck in parts of Europe, the hardy and nutritious tuber saved the populace from starvation.

Pumpkin

Pumpkins have an abundance of seeds inside, which connect them with fertility, creativity, and abundance. Toast the seeds in the oven, then add them to talismans for prosperity. If you want to get pregnant, fill a charm bag with the seeds and sleep with it under your pillow. Artists can eat the seeds to gain inspiration.

You see pumpkins everywhere in October, as the wheel turns toward Samhain and Halloween. Centuries ago, people in Ireland carved ghoulish faces in turnips to scare off evil spirits. Immigrants brought the custom across the Atlantic and traded out turnips for the pumpkins native to North America. Kitchen witches know that spirits abound at Samhain, but you don't necessarily want to chase them away. Instead, this is the best time of the year to commune with loved ones and helpers on the other side. Maybe you'd rather attract the help of benevolent spirits by carving a pumpkin with images that represent what you desire. Put a candle inside, then place the pumpkin on your altar or in another prominent spot during a Samhain ritual.

If you use pumpkin to bake a holiday pumpkin pie, spice it with cinnamon for prosperity, nutmeg for good luck and intuition, and allspice for success. Samhain is also the perfect time to pull out your cauldron and brew up a magic pumpkin soup. Stir in cumin and coconut milk for protection. Snip fresh mint to attract money and grate ginger to speed the spell's action, then sprinkle them on top of the soup and add a dollop of plain Greek yogurt.

Raspberry

Ruled by Venus—the planet that governs women, love, and relationships—raspberries are a favorite ingredient in love magic. The fruit's deep red juice brings to mind blood and the heart. Therefore, kitchen witches can use raspberries (fresh or dried) as well as their leaves in spells to attract a new lover, strengthen a loving bond between partners, or soothe a broken heart after a loss or disappointment. Christianity connects the berry with kindness, which stems from the heart. You can even substitute raspberry juice in spells that call for writing with blood.

Witches link the color red with passion, hence raspberries have long been included in charms to heat up a flagging romance. If your libido has diminished due to menopause, childbirth, illness, or medications, consider adding raspberries to your diet. For centuries, natural healers have relied on this pretty fruit to aid women during pregnancy and childbirth, as well as for menstrual problems and menopause. Each berry is made up of a hundred or so bead-like seeds, known as drupelets, which gives raspberries their reputation for encouraging fertility in women. Combine raspberries with other fruits—strawberries, blueberries, peaches, bananas—in salads, desserts, or smoothies to fine-tune your spells.

Rice

Associated with love, fertility, and happiness, rice is tossed by well-wishers at weddings. Although people usually throw white rice, red rice is a better choice because the color symbolizes passion, enthusiasm, and vitality. Folklore tells us this practice keeps evil spirits away too—the spirits will accept the rice as a bribe and leave the newly married couple alone. Rice can provide protection in other ways too. Fill a charm bag with dried rice and carry it in your pocket to keep you safe. Sprinkle grains of rice in a circle around your home or on the roof to protect the occupants and your property. White or black rice—or a combination of the two—is best for protection spells.

Centuries ago, rice served as a form of currency in China and India. Kitchen witches can still use it in prosperity spells. Make a magical Mexican pilaf with green rice, poblano peppers, cilantro, parsley, onion, and garlic to bring quick cash. Or cook yellow rice, which gets its golden color from turmeric and/or saffron, to attract wealth. Snip a bit of fresh parsley, cilantro, or mint on top to add extra flavor and money-drawing power.

Archaeologists believe rice has been cultivated for almost ten thousand years, but it didn't arrive in Europe until much later. Some sources say Alexander the Great brought it to Greece about 2,400 years ago. The Spanish began cultivating it in the eighth century. Rice only became an established crop in America during the colonial period. A staple food for billions of people in India, China, Japan, and other parts of Asia, it's played a role in every aspect of life: the economy, community development, wars, religion, and social customs.

Rosemary

Considered a woman's herb, rosemary has long been grown by kitchen witches for both culinary and magic purposes. The fragrant herb is said to represent the matriarch of the home and the dominance of feminine power. Mythology links the herb with the Greek goddess Aphrodite, one of the deities of love, beauty, and fertility. But Aphrodite wasn't just another pretty face—she also supported the arts, culture, and knowledge in its many expressions.

Rosemary possesses properties that witches can use to benefit their creativity and intellectual pursuits. Ancient Greek scholars wore garlands of rosemary on their heads to strengthen their memories. Modern-day kitchen witches can tap the mind-boosting powers of rosemary, too, in their craft. Put a bowl of potpourri that contains rosemary by your desk, where its pungent fragrance will keep you mentally sharp. Add it to a talisman and carry it with you when you need your intellect to function at its peak.

Witches also consider rosemary a multibeneficial plant, and as the old saying goes, rosemary should be planted by the garden gate to bring good luck. One reason for this is that rosemary's strong scent deters insect pests. Hang a bundle of the herb at your front door to scare away other "pests" as well.

Rye

Ruled by Venus, the planet astrologers associate with love and relationships, rye has long been a component of spells for fidelity and permanence in love. Because the grain is winter hardy and can grow in poor soil, it signifies endurance and the ability to hang in there during hard times as well as good. Bake pumpernickel or dark rye bread to strengthen commitment in a romantic relationship if you feel a partner may be losing interest or your relationship is rocky. Inscribe hearts, *X*'s (*gebo*, the rune symbol for relationships), or other images that represent love in the crust and share the bread with your beloved.

Rye is native to southwestern Asia and has been cultivated there for thousands of years. It found its way to the Balkan region, where it became popular for making rye whiskey, as a cereal grain, for livestock feed, and even for thatching. Tie a bunch of dried rye stalks together and hang them in your kitchen to promote affection, trust, and harmony in your home. Braid three stalks to bring courage, patience, and perseverance during challenging times. Put rye seeds in a charm bag and tie it with eight knots—eight is the number of permanence.

Saffron

This precious botanical derives from the delicate stigmas of the saffron crocus flower (each flower has only three), and it's the most expensive spice in the world. Not surprisingly, kitchen witches use it in prosperity magic—its imagery clearly expresses what the spells seek to attract.

Once used as a dye for royal robes (and now associated with the garments of Buddhist monks), golden saffron can be mixed in water and used to paint magic sigils, symbols, and other images on paper for spellcraft. You can also draw "tattoos" on your skin with the saffron dye to reinforce your intention. Saffron's color brings to mind the life-giving power of the sun; therefore, you may want to include it in workings for recognition, leadership, and career success. The bright yellow-orange color reminds one of gold—a universal marker of wealth—and as witches know, symbolism is important in magic.

Because wealth is often associated with power, and power is a heady aphrodisiac, saffron also has a place in love spells. Include it in Indian food and share the meal with a lover (or potential romantic partner) to spark passion.

Sage

Among magic workers, sage is one of the most popular herbs for purification and cleansing. Witches often burn it to remove unwanted influences and energies from a space where a spell or ritual will take place. Before people enter a magic circle, they may be blessed and cleansed by smoke from a sage wand. It's customary to purify ritual tools before using them to perform magic; one popular way to do this is by holding the tool in the smoke of burning sage. You can also burn sage to clear bad vibes from your home after an argument or disruption and to remove another person's energy from objects you acquire, especially jewelry or antique furniture.

Sage is a perennial herb used to flavor many soups, stews, casseroles, and meat and fish dishes. Its name comes from the Latin word *salveo*, which means "to heal" or "to save." The ancient Romans considered sage a sacred herb of immortality. The term *sage* also refers to a wise person, which gives clues to the plant's inner nature. In addition to the soft, gray-green leafy variety used in cooking, sage comes in purple, blue, gold, white, and red versions, each with its own unique characteristics. Indigenous people of the North American plains and holistic healers praise its antibacterial and purifying qualities, which can treat skin problems including acne, rashes, and eczema.

Salt

Salt's purifying and protective properties make it a favorite substance for magic spells. Add Epsom or sea salts to a ritual bath to cleanse yourself in preparation for magic work. Sprinkle a pinch of salt in each corner of a room to ward off unwanted energies and cleanse the area. Wash an object with salt water to purify it (wash metal items with sweet water, however, because salt can tarnish or corrode them).

So essential is salt to health and well-being that this mineral was used for thousands of years as a form of currency—and still is in some parts of the world. The phrase *worth his salt* derives from the practice of bartering slaves for salt, and the English word *salary* comes from the Latin *salarius*, meaning "of or relating to salt." *Salt of the earth* refers to someone who's respected in the community, a pillar of society.

Salt is also a common, inexpensive, and widely used ingredient for food preservation; before modern refrigeration, it enabled people to store meat, fish, and vegetables for long periods of time. Although today salt-restricted diets are often recommended to lower blood pressure and reduce the risk of stroke or coronary problems, few cooks would willingly banish salt from the meals they prepare.

Savory

Native to the Mediterranean region, savory comes in both summer and winter varieties. Summer savory has a reputation among kitchen witches as an ingredient for love potions. In Greek and Roman mythology, satyrs—horned and hairy goat-like deities known for their lusty natures—wore garlands of savory on their heads, perhaps to enhance their sexual prowess. Artists sometimes depict the nature god Pan wearing savory in his hair. The winter type, however, produces the opposite effect, so make sure you choose the right one according to your intention! Brew fresh summer savory in a tea and drink it to spark desire. If you wish to quell the ardor of an unwanted suitor, give that person a potion made with winter savory. You can also include the herb in spells to end a romantic relationship.

Medicinally, savory has been used for centuries by herbalists in syrups to soothe sore throats and coughs, ease colic, and clear nasal congestion. As an essential oil, the herb can bring relief from skin irritations including psoriasis and eczema.

Spearmint

A member of the mint family, refreshing spearmint is one of the most popular all-purpose money-drawing herbs. Grow spearmint in a pot on a kitchen windowsill so you'll have the fresh herb available for cooking and magic work.

Spearmint's cleansing and purifying properties help remove energetic blocks that may be interfering with your prosperity. Burn the dried leaves and let the smoke waft through your home to clear away bad vibes. Add dried spearmint to talismans or charm bags to attract wealth, or put some in an amulet with a piece of snowflake obsidian to protect your finances. Kitchen witches also use spearmint to promote clear thinking, improve memory, and focus the mind when working spells—and we all know how important focus is in magic. The herb can enhance psychic vision too.

Crush fresh leaves with your fingertips, then inhale the crisp scent to stimulate intuition.

Brew spearmint tea and drink it to aid digestion, ease nausea, or relieve bloating. A natural antioxidant with antibacterial properties, the herb promotes good oral health; add it to toothpaste or mouthwash. Chew spearmint gum to clean your breath and remind you of your magic intentions. It also makes a delicious garnish with hummus or baba ghanoush. Snip the fresh herb on salads; cold, creamy vegetable soups; and rice dishes.

Spinach

Kitchen witches can cook up spells with spinach to gain strength physically, emotionally, or intellectually. If your goal is to strengthen your financial situation, spinach is a good choice. Like other green foods, it represents money—especially in the US, where dollar bills are green. Dry the leaves to use in prosperity talismans. Shred or cut a dollar bill (or another denomination or currency) into tiny pieces and mix it with dried, crumbled spinach leaves, then scatter them near the entrance of your home to attract wealth.

Spinach is native to Persia—the word means "green hand" in Persian. Arab traders brought it to Europe, where it became popular in Italy during the Renaissance thanks to Catherine de Medici's habit of eating it with every meal. Not only is spinach great for salads and green smoothies, it can also be incorporated into a wide variety of dishes from countries around the world. Spinach also contains both calcium and magnesium for healthy bones, plus iron and vitamins A and C.

Squash

To understand squash's correspondences in spellcraft, you need to consider its characteristics. More than a hundred dred different types of squash exist, both summer and winter varieties. Zucchini and yellow summer squash proliferate during warm months—their rapid, plentiful growth makes them a natural in spells for abundance. Hardy acorn and butternut squashes, which ripen when the weather grows cooler, have a place in spells for endurance, strength, protection, and longevity.

The symbolism of the shapes and colors (as discussed in Chapter 4) of the squashes is important too. The phallic shape of zucchini and yellow squash represents masculine energy and fertility, so these vegetables can be used in spells to increase male virility, vitality, and libido. Acorn squash, pumpkin, and spaghetti squash, on the other hand, more closely resemble the womb; therefore, they can benefit spells for women. Consider orange varieties, such as butternut squash, when you want to inspire creativity, joy, and enthusiasm. Delicate squash blossoms can help you deal with sensitive issues or become kinder and gentler.

Strawberry

Like raspberries, strawberries symbolize love and happiness in romantic relationships. The pretty red fruit resembles a heart, which—according to sympathetic magic—makes it ideal for love spells. To heighten romance, affection, and lust with a partner, melt dark chocolate in a saucepan. Sprinkle in a little cinnamon to increase the heat and stir with a wooden spoon in a clockwise direction. Then dip fresh strawberries in the chocolate and feed them to each other in the moonlight. Or share a hot fudge sundae made with strawberry ice cream.

You can also put dried strawberries and/or their leaves in love talismans, include strawberry juice in love potions, and mix a few drops of strawberry essential oil into a love lotion or add them to a romantic bath.

According to Greek mythology, strawberries grew from the blood of Adonis, who died in the arms of his beloved Aphrodite after being gored by a wild boar. A Cherokee tale says strawberries healed a quarrel between First Woman and First Man, thus enabling the human race to evolve.

Sugar

Sugar is a key ingredient in the kitchen witch's toolbox. Without it, you wouldn't have candy, cookies, pies, cakes, ice cream, and all the other delicious desserts that give your life a welcome touch of sweetness. For kitchen witches, sugar is more than a flavoring in many favorite recipes—it also finds its way into most love spells.

One of the most common and enjoyable kitchen witch love spells is to bake a sweet, luscious, maybe a bit decadent dessert for a lover. Chocolate comes to mind, for chocolate is the property of the love goddess Aphrodite. (It's no coincidence that people give chocolates on Valentine's Day as an expression of love.) If you've decided to eschew sugar in your diet, you can still gain its benefits in your magical workings. Sprinkle a poppet (identified as your beloved) with sugar water to inspire affection in the object of your desire. Add sugar to bathwater and soak in it prior to a romantic ritual. Include a sugar cube in a charm bag and set it in the relationships gua of your home to attract love (see the section on feng shui in Chapter 4).

In recent years, sugar has gotten a bad rap, mostly because people tend to overindulge in it, which can lead to obesity, diabetes, and other health problems. But sugar, extracted from the sugarcane plant, has been part of humankind's diet for millennia.

Sunflower Seeds

With their big, showy golden blooms, sunflowers often remind people of the sun, hence their name. Astrologers connect the Sun with fame and fortune, leadership and respect, and creativity and self-expression. If any of these things is on your agenda, sunflower seeds have a place in your magic work. The seeds hold the potential to help you achieve success in any endeavor you set your mind to. They also signify abundance—look at how many seeds a single flower contains.

Just seeing sunflowers is enough to make some people feel happy, so kitchen witches may want to display them in their homes to encourage joy and congeniality. They're a bright and beautiful addition to summer solstice gatherings—or any occasion, for that matter. Include the seeds in charm bags to lift someone's spirits or to bolster self-confidence.

The Indigenous people of North America began cultivating sunflowers for food more than 4,500 ago—every part of the plant can be eaten. Sunflowers follow the sun as it moves across the sky, turning from east in the morning to west in the afternoon. Add the seeds to an amulet when you're traveling to ensure your journey will be pleasant. Birds love them too, so share sunflower seeds with your feathered friends.

Tarragon

Nicknamed "nature's little dragon" because its roots look like snakes, tarragon has a time-honored place in banishing spells. On a piece of paper, write what you want to eliminate, then fold the paper around a pinch of tarragon and burn it. It's also an herb of protection—combine it with basil in amulets or grow the two plants together in a witchy window box to safeguard a home and its inhabitants.

Perhaps oddly, tarragon blends the powers to repel and attract. In love spells, it puts an end to lingering bad feelings left over from an unhappy relationship in the past so you can go on to find new love. In money spells, it clears old attitudes about unworthiness and enables you to attract the prosperity you deserve. Artists and writers can use tarragon to overcome creative blocks and self-judgment and open up to new ideas and inspiration. And if you're having trouble sleeping, tarragon's calming energy may reduce stress, quiet restless thinking, and encourage pleasant dreams.

In terms of cooking, this fragrant herb supposedly found its way from Russia to Europe during the Middle Ages, where it took up permanent residence in popular French sauces such as béarnaise and hollandaise. Tarragon is also a delicious addition to chicken and fish dishes, as well as vegetables.

Thyme

This popular culinary herb is a favorite among kitchen witches for both its distinctive flavor and its magical qualities. Valued for its protective and purifying properties, thyme is a good choice for clearing sacred or ritual space. Burn the dried leaves as you would sage and let the smoke waft through the area to remove unwanted energies. You can also cleanse ritual tools in the smoke.

Ruled by Venus, the planet astrologers connect with love and relationships, thyme is a good choice for love spells. It invites cooperation, affection, and happiness between romantic partners and among family members. To promote congeniality, hang bunches of thyme in rooms where people gather. Put dried thyme in talismans to attract love. Fashion a tiny besom from a bunch of thyme leaves, then "sweep" the air in a room after an argument. Blend the powdered herb in a lotion and rub it on your heart to ease sadness and restore optimism after a disappointment.

In cooking, thyme is a natural pairing with chicken dishes, potatoes, legumes, and soups. According to folklore, fairies and nature spirits have a fondness for thyme, so it's good to plant it in a garden where it will draw these helpers to bless your vegetables, fruits, and flowers.

Tomato

The bright red color of the most popular varieties of tomatoes means this fruit is often associated with love and passion. The French sometimes refer to the tomato as the *pomme d'amour*, meaning "love apple." If you want to encourage inspiration, passion, and creativity in a romantic partnership, eat tomatoes raw or cooked. Tomatoes combine both sweet and slightly sour flavors, aptly symbolizing the nature of most love relationships.

For two centuries, beginning in the 1700s, people in England and parts of Europe were afraid to eat tomatoes and labeled them "poison apples." However, the tomato wasn't to blame for the deaths that followed its consumption—the lead plates from which people ate this acidic fruit caused the problem. Early immigrants to the Americas feared tomatoes for another reason. They're part of the nightshade family (along with bell peppers and eggplants), which includes the toxic belladonna, known as the "deadly nightshade." The Aztecs, though, had been safely enjoying tomatoes for nearly a millennium before the fruit arrived in Spain with the conquistadors. Fortunately, people now know tomatoes are a great source of vitamin C and can aid your immune system.

Turmeric

Turmeric's brilliant golden orange color is a clue to its uses in kitchen witchery and magic in general. Let turmeric inspire courage and self-confidence when you face a challenge. Dissolve the powdered herb in water, then paint a sigil with it that conveys your purpose. If you like, you can paint the sigil on fresh-baked bread or another food, then incorporate your intention into your body as you eat. We associate the Sun with vitality, creative power, and masculine energy. Use this sunny herb when you need a little extra oomph to achieve your goals. Turmeric's color is also reminiscent of gold, so you can include the herb in money spells too.

A popular spice in Indian cuisine for millenia, turmeric gives a distinctive flavor to curries, dals, and saag. Much of spellcraft relies on symbolism, and colors trigger associations that witches can tap for specific purposes (see Chapter 4 for more about this). In India, for instance, gold and orange marigolds represent happiness, passion, creativity, and divine blessings. In other parts of the world as well, bright golden orange reminds one of the sun and its life-giving nature. Therefore, kitchen witches can draw upon solar imagery when working with this herb.

A natural antioxidant, turmeric protects against damage caused by free radicals and is considered beneficial for people with heart conditions and diabetes.

Valerian

Historically, valerian has been known as a witch's herb, though today most people think of it as an aid to relaxation and sleep. A powerful protection herb, it was used by the early Greeks to chase away evil spirits. The Celts believed it kept them safe from lightning. You, too, can hang valerian above the entrance to your home to guard against unwanted intruders (physical or nonphysical), accidents, and injuries. Put the herb in a protection amulet and carry it in your pocket or purse, or store some in your car's glove compartment for safe journeys.

Also considered an herb of communication—it's ruled by the planet Mercury, which astrologers say governs communication—valerian can encourage congenial discussions between people. Its soothing properties calm the emotions and ease tensions that can lead to arguments. You can also use the herb to focus your mind when you want to connect with helpers in the spirit realm or receive insights from your higher self. Drink valerian tea at bedtime to induce sleep (you can purchase the herb in capsules too). Herbal healers also blend valerian in salves to reduce muscle tension and relieve minor aches and pains.

Vanilla

Kitchen witches know there's nothing "plain" about vanilla. Vanilla is a popular ingredient in love spells. One reason is that vanilla calms fears and judgments, replacing them with soothing, nurturing feelings of acceptance. Instead of stimulating your emotions, it supports them and gives you a sense that all is well. The result is a joyful, lighthearted approach to love and affection, rather than grand passion. Combine vanilla with chocolate (as in a hot fudge sundae), and you've got the makings for romance.

Vanilla incense or candles scented with vanilla can bring a peaceful ambience to a ritual setting. Burn them to enhance meditation and relaxation. Vanilla essential oil added to bathwater or soap can help you unwind at bedtime and enjoy pleasant dreams.

This delicious spice is well known as a flavoring in ice cream, cakes and cookies, puddings and custards, and all manner of edible goodies. It's one of the most expensive spices in the world (surpassed by saffron), and yet it's one of the most widely used in the world of desserts. Its warm, sensual, comforting aroma invites you to relax, indulge, and enjoy the good things in life.

Vinegar

You're probably aware of vinegar's cleansing properties when it comes to washing windows and floors. As a kitchen witch, you can transform those everyday chores into magic spells, and vinegar can help. Before performing a spell or ritual, clean the surfaces where you'll work with a vinegar-and-water

solution (rub in a counterclockwise direction to banish). This natural puri-
fier removes dirt, grime, and unwanted energies from your sacred space—
and it's safe for children and pets.

The use of vinegar in banishing spells dates back thousands of years
to the ancient Babylonians. Kitchen witches still turn to vinegar for protection spells. Mix white vinegar with water in a spray bottle and spritz
your home, your office, or another area you wish to safeguard. Add it to
bathwater to clear disruptive psychic influences or to ease the effects of an
emotional upset.

During the medieval period in Europe, people used balsamic vinegar
as a disinfectant and tonic for colds, sore throats, and other maladies.
Today, it's considered useful for lowering cholesterol. Apple cider vinegar
is a wonderful digestive aid that, despite its sharp, sour taste, balances your
system.

Wheat

Wheat has been a staple in the diets of people around the
world and has nourished us for so long (archaeologists estimate
we've been eating it for ten thousand years) that many kitchen
witches consider it a "sacred grain." Ceres, the goddess of grain crops,
agriculture, and fertility, occupied an exalted place in the Roman pantheon. In early cultures, the wheat harvest determined whether communities thrived or starved; therefore, wheat became associated with life, death,
and rebirth. On August 1, Wiccans and other pagans celebrate the first
of the harvest festivals, Lughnasad, also known as *Lammas*, which means
"loaf mass." Bake your favorite bread and put a dried pea in the dough.
Whoever gets the pea will be granted a wish.

Wheat is linked with gold, wealth, and abundance of all kinds due to its golden color. In many parts of Europe, our ancestors hung sheaves of wheat near the doors to their homes to attract prosperity—you can too. Include dried wheat in talismans or charm bags to draw money to you. You may want to fashion a kitchen witch poppet out of wheat stalks to bring good luck to your home. *Bread* and *dough* are even slang words for money.

In ancient Greece, newly married couples wore headdresses made of wheat to encourage a happy, fruitful relationship. To bless a union, consider showering a bride and groom with wheat kernels instead of rice. Baked goods made with wheat and sugar (or honey) can encourage affectionate feelings, especially if you decorate your cakes, cookies, etc. with symbols of love and share them with your partner.

Today, wheat is the world's most traded crop and figures prominently in the diets of people around the globe as bread, pasta, cereal, confectionary, pancakes, and on and on. The common terms in our vernacular for wheat and bread show how important this grain has been to humanity over the ages. For example, *the staff of life* indicates how vital wheat is as a food crop; *breaking bread* with friends, family, and neighbors recognizes the value of community and comradeship.

Yam

Like other root crops, yams (and sweet potatoes) can help you stay grounded when life seems out of control. Sweeter than white potatoes, they can stabilize romantic relationships, family connections, and friendships and help you establish harmony and trust with the people you love. If you have a garden, plant this vegetable for security in the domestic arena. Eating yams can also show you how to enjoy more sweetness in your everyday life. Witches associate their orange color with enthusiasm and joy, so instead of hash browns, eat yams at breakfast to start the day on a bright note.

African legends say the Yoruban healer-protector goddess Aja created yams, which are an important staple in the diets of people in Nigeria. An African creation story bears similarities to the story of the Garden of Eden in Genesis, except the forbidden fruit was a yam instead of an apple. The creator god, Ruwa, gave humans a perfect existence in paradise so long as they didn't eat one particular edible root, the yam. When they disobeyed, Ruwa made them mortal.

Part 4

Common Spells, Charms, and Rituals for Kitchen Witches

In this part, you will find spells and charms common to the kitchen witch's practice. It is essential that you understand the herbs or other edibles you will be using in your spells, so be sure to research them thoroughly using either Part 3 of this book or your other reference books. If you have grown your own herbs or are out foraging for some, don't collect an entire plant. Take only what you need—the old adage *less is more* should be at the forefront of your thoughts. Also, in many of these spells and rituals, you can choose the amount of the herbs and spices you add, so be mindful of that when harvesting. Remember also that when you harvest plant matter, an exchange of energy occurs, so be sure to bring something as an offering to the plant, perhaps some water, and thank the plant for sharing its bounty with you.

You will also find in this part advice and instructions for candle spells, making bath salts and teas, cleaning your home magically, and making talismans, amulets, poppets, and more. Remember to keep your intentions in mind as you go about performing your spells and rituals to help infuse your purposes into the objects you are creating or cooking.

A Clean Sweep

You're surely familiar with the stereotypical image of a witch riding a broomstick, but in reality witches don't use brooms to fly through the sky. They use brooms, or besoms, for sweeping, just like other folks do. However, kitchen witches don't only sweep up dirt and dust in their homes—they get rid of unwanted energies and bad vibes at the same time. You'll want to perform this cleansing and clearing task before a ritual, ceremony, or spellworking.

Materials Needed

* 1 besom or regular broom

Steps to Take

1. Begin in the easternmost part of the area you plan to clean and start sweeping.
2. Move in a counterclockwise direction, using your broom to sweep not only the floor but the air around you as well. You may want to chant, sing, or recite an affirmation that states your intention as you sweep.
3. While you work, envision all harmful, disruptive, and imbalanced energies being whisked away.
4. Continue sweeping in this manner until you feel your space is free of anything that might interfere with your magic.

Let the Sun Shine In

We associate light and sunshine with ideas, clarity, and happiness. Dirty windows that inhibit sunlight from illuminating your home symbolically limit your ability to see clearly too. If you're having trouble understanding a situation, person, or issue, washing windows may help you gain insight. This task can also give you a brighter outlook on life.

Materials Needed

- 1 (20–24-ounce) spray bottle
- 2 cups distilled water
- ½ cup white vinegar or rubbing alcohol
- Cleaning cloth(s) or paper towels

Steps to Take

1. Wash the spray bottle. Pour the distilled water into the bottle.
2. Add the vinegar or rubbing alcohol to the water. Shake to blend.
3. Wash as many windows as you feel like doing.
4. While you work, focus your attention on your intention. Allow your mind to remain open and be confident that you'll receive insight, information, or guidance that will help you resolve the matter that concerns you.

Clear the Air

After an argument or upsetting experience, clear away the bad vibes lingering in your home to restore peace and harmony. This is also a good practice after you've had workers in your home or when you move into a new place to remove other people's energies.

Materials Needed

- 1 (16–24-ounce) spray bottle
- 2 cups spring water
- 3 drops lemon essential oil
- 3 drops lavender essential oil

Steps to Take

1. Wash the spray bottle. Pour the spring water into the bottle.
2. Add the lemon essential oil to the water. Lemon has cleansing properties and a refreshing scent that remove unpleasant energies.
3. Add the lavender essential oil to the mixture. Lavender's soothing scent calms tensions and restores harmony.
4. Shake the bottle to blend the ingredients.
5. Mist the room(s) with the fragrant mixture to clear and balance the air.
6. While you work, envision all unwanted energies being neutralized and peaceful ones filling the space. You may want to chant, sing, or repeat an affirmation that states your intention, or play relaxing music.

Metal Magic

In astrology, everything on earth falls into the domain of one or more of the celestial bodies. Each of the planets and lights has its own unique properties. Kitchen witches can draw on planetary energies by cooking and serving food in pots, pans, and dishes made of metals that correspond to their intentions.

Materials Needed

- Cookware, dishes, cutlery, and so on made of the metal that corresponds to your intentions

Steps to Take

1. Gold is ruled by the Sun. The Sun holds the center of our solar neighborhood and oversees authority, fatherhood, vitality, honor, success, power, and healing. If your intention involves one or more of these things, use gold-colored pots, pans, and cookware. Serve meals on gold plates, drink from golden cups, and eat with gold-plated utensils. Decorate foods with edible gold foil.

2. Silver is ruled by the Moon. The Moon governs home, family, motherhood, women, fertility, the emotions, and intuition. If your intention involves one or more of these things, use silver (or silver-plated) cutlery to eat your meals. Silver goblets, salt and pepper shakers, serving bowls, and other accessories also infuse food with the Moon's vibrations.

3. Copper is ruled by Venus, the planet astrologers connect with love, romantic and business relationships, women, the arts, creativity, harmony, and prosperity. If your intention involves one or more of these things, use copper pots and pans for cooking, or heat water for a magic tea in a copper kettle. Serve food in copper bowls with copper utensils to infuse it with Venus's vibrations.

4. Iron falls into the domain of Mars, the planet that governs men, athletics, competition, passion, assertiveness, courage, and war. If your intention involves one or more of these things, use iron pots, pans, and skillets for cooking. Bake muffins in a cast iron pan. Heat water in an iron kettle. Make a stew or roast in a cast iron cauldron or Dutch oven to infuse it with Mars's vibrations.

5. Tin is ruled by Jupiter. The largest planet in our solar system, Jupiter is linked with growth, good luck, expansion, abundance, higher knowledge, spirituality, and long-distance travel. If your intention involves one or more of these things, use tin (or tin-lined) pots and pans for cooking. Store food in tin containers. Eat with tin utensils. Drink from tin cups to infuse beverages with Jupiter's vibrations.

6. Lead is ruled by Saturn. Saturn, as the last of the classical planets, rules time, fate, boundaries, ancestors, restrictions, funerals, and endings of all kinds. However, lead is poisonous! If your intention involves one or more of these things, utilize antique china serving dishes with a clear glass dish on top. It's okay to put leaded crystal candlesticks on your table, but don't drink from leaded crystal goblets. Include lead serving trays or table decorations that never come into direct contact with your food and drinks. Utilize lead dishes and cups for meals offered exclusively to the dead.

7. As you serve and eat your meals, keep your intentions in mind. If you are dining with other people, discuss your objectives and how you might bring them to fruition. Give thanks to the gods and goddesses associated with the planets and lights for their assistance.

Stir the Pot

Stir the Pot You're likely familiar with the practice of casting a circle by moving in a clockwise direction and opening it again by moving counterclockwise. But did you know clockwise movements can also be used to attract or increase, whereas counterclockwise ones can repel or diminish? This magic technique works best when you're making stews, soups, and other dishes that require a lot of stirring over a period of time, such as polenta.

Materials Needed

- 1 or more pots, pans, and/or bowls (made of a material that corresponds to your intention)
- 1 or more spoons, preferably wooden or metal (not plastic)

Steps to Take

1. While you're cooking, focus on your objective and what you intend to manifest. Keep your intention in mind as you stir whatever you're making. Your thoughts will be absorbed by the food you're preparing and subsequently incorporated into the bodies of those who eat it.

2. If your goal is to attract or increase something in your life—love, money, success, good health, friends—stir in a clockwise direction.

3. If your goal is to repel or decrease something in your life, stir in a counterclockwise direction.

4. Three is the number witches use to seal a spell and bring it into manifestation in the three-dimensional world. Therefore, you'll want to stir whatever you're cooking three times. Repeat as often as necessary, using three circles each time.

5. You can also use this magical technique when mixing batter for cake, cookies, or other baked goods; stirring milk or sugar into coffee or tea; and combining salad dressing into vegetables.

Circular Cleaning
Witches can take the symbolism of using circular movements in magic work (as discussed in the previous entry) into areas beyond the kitchen and apply it to other tasks. For kitchen witches, every facet of domestic life is imbued with power, and the everyday world is integrally connected to the mystical one. When you view household jobs as sacred expressions of your role as a witch, even the lowliest chore has magical possibilities.

Materials Needed
- Cleaning supplies (will vary)

Steps to Take
1. When you're washing up after a meal, scrub dishes, pots, and pans in clockwise circles to encourage attraction or increase. To bring about decrease or to repel something, wash with counterclockwise motions.
2. Clean the bathroom sink, bathtub, and toilet in clockwise circles to encourage attraction or increase. To bring about decrease or to repel something, wash them with counterclockwise motions.
3. Polish furniture, wipe countertops, vacuum, dust, wash windows, sweep, and so on in a circular manner to foster your intentions.

Purifying Floor Wash
Washing your floors may feel like the least witchy thing you could do, but magical floor washes are an intrinsic part of kitchen witch skills. They combine physical house cleaning with spiritual and magical work. Furthermore, they are a discreet way to practice magic without advertising your intentions, so if you are still in the "broom closet," magical floor washes may be a powerful way for you to cast spells without anyone knowing! They are common in magical traditions like Brujeria, hoodoo, and Yoruba. A floor wash should be a final rinse applied to floors that have already been cleaned, and it should be allowed to remain on the floors until it air-dries. This allows the magic to permeate into the surrounding atmosphere. Washes provide an extra layer of protection and an energetic seal when doing your monthly or seasonal cleansing routines.

Materials Needed
- Bucket
- Warm water (to fill bucket)
- 2–3 pinches sea salt
- 1 cup white vinegar
- Rosemary, fresh or dried
- Orange peels, fresh or dried
- Lemon peels, fresh or dried
- Hyssop, fresh or dried
- Eucalyptus leaves, fresh or dried

Steps to Take
1. Fill your bucket with warm water. Add a few pinches of salt.
2. Add vinegar and a generous handful of rosemary, orange peels, lemon peels, hyssop, and eucalyptus.
3. Envision a white or gold light running down your arm and into the water. See the water radiating with light.
4. Mop or wash your floors with your charged floor wash, and enjoy the magical energies.

Spice It Up
Including herbs in spell casting is a fundamental part of the witch's craft. Herbs and spices contain energies from the sun and earth and can imbue your spells with the energies of the elements, the directions, and the planets. This applies to the food you cook. Charging your herbs and spices makes every meal a magical feast.

Materials Needed
- Your herb and spice collection
- 1 white candle, any size
- Matches or lighter
- 1 dried bay leaf

Steps to Take
1. Gather your spice collection. Light your candle. Take three deep breaths, centering and grounding your energy into the moment.
2. Light the tip of the bay leaf and then blow it out, letting it smolder. Trail the smoke over the outside of one of the containers to cleanse the container and the herbs inside of any residual, unwanted energies. Bay leaf was sacred to the Greek god Apollo who is associated with the sun, and this practice evokes the solar power of this deity.
3. Quickly pass the container over the flame of the candle. Hold the container in both hands and envision a golden light passing from your hands into your container of herbs. Allow the space of three heartbeats to pass. Repeat with each spice container.
4. Now, every time you cook with these spices, you are sprinkling that energy directly into your food.
5. Once you have "spiced up" the dry herbs, bring this same intention to the liquid spices, like your extracts, food colorings, oils, and vinegars.
6. You can also push this idea even further by cleansing and energizing the very shelves or cupboard where you store your spices.

Create Affirmations or Incantations

You've learned already about affirmations and the magical power they have. Affirmations are short, positive statements worded in the present tense to bring about a result you desire. Incantations are affirmations that have a rhyme and rhythm and are perhaps set to music. For example:

"As the day fades into night
"I draw a love that's good and right.
"As the night turns into day
"We are blessed in every way."

Materials Needed

❧ None

Steps to Take

1. Say your affirmation or incantation each morning upon entering your kitchen. Say it again each night when you turn off the kitchen light and head for bed.

2. Repeat your affirmation or incantation daily until your intention manifests or you choose to focus on another matter.

3. If you like, write down your affirmation or incantation and display it in a spot where you'll see it often, such as on your refrigerator. You could even get a refrigerator magnet printed with it. You could also consider having your affirmation or incantation printed on a coffee mug, so every time you drink from it you'll be reminded of your intention.

Herbal Amulet to Protect Your Home This

amulet protects your home from intruders, nosy neighbors, and people you'd rather not have around. You can also use it to safeguard your home from nonphysical beings who don't have your best interests at heart. If your goal is to ward off fairies (who have a tendency to steal stuff, especially crystals and jewelry), add an iron nail to each pouch. While this recipe covers how to make one amulet pouch, you should make one of these pouches for each exterior door of your home.

Materials Needed

- 1 pinch dried basil leaves
- 1 pinch fennel seeds
- 1 pinch dried oregano leaves
- 1 pinch dried rosemary sprigs
- 1 pinch dried tarragon
- 1 pinch dried or powdered valerian
- Black drawstring pouch, preferably made of silk or leather

Steps to Take

1. Put a pinch of each botanical into the black pouch.
2. Tie the pouch shut with eight knots. Eight is the number of banishing.
3. While you tie the knots, say this incantation (or one you compose yourself) aloud:

   "From energies I don't invite
   "This spell protects me day and night."

4. Hang the pouch on the inside of each exterior door of your home to provide protection. Envision yourself safe and sound, completely surrounded by a sphere of pure white light that no one can penetrate without your permission.

Flower Divination
Victorian witches practiced this fun and simple form of divination with spring wildflowers. This spell only requires some time to wander outside and a basket to collect your flowers. Though wildflowers typically blossom in spring, this spell can be worked any time there are wildflowers in bloom near you.

Materials Needed
- Wildflowers
- Basket
- Guidebook for identifying flowers
- Time to take a stroll

Steps to Take
1. Grab your basket and head out for a walk in an area with plenty of flowers in bloom.
2. Once there, close your eyes and take a few deep breaths to center and ground yourself.
3. Open your heart to Mother Nature and whatever messages the universe may have for you, or if you have a specific question, concentrate and repeat the question to yourself three times. Three is a magical number witches frequently use in spellwork.
4. Open your eyes and pick the first three different flowers that you see. If you want, continue to pick more flowers for a lovely bouquet, but keep those first three separate.

5. When you get home, use your guidebook to identify the flowers, then look up the magical meanings of each. That is the answer to your question. For example:

Friendship and happiness	sweet pea, tuberose, morning glory, passionflower
Love and lust	lemon verbena, joe-pye weed, daisy, cattail, violet, nettle, forget-me-not
Wisdom	coralroot, sunflower, coltsfoot, sage
Protection	black-eyed Susan, parsnip, heather, mullein, honeysuckle, bee balm
Money matters	vervain, periwinkle, blackberry, goldenrod, buttercup
Wishes and luck	bluebell, clover, dandelion, fire wheel
Healing	burdock, milkweed, wild mint, Saint-John's-wort, knotweed
Courage	columbine, yarrow, ragweed, wild thyme, wood lily

Herbal Love Potpourri
This pretty blend of herbs and spices combines botanicals for love and affection in a romantic relationship. Each herb or spice brings its individual qualities to the mix: star anise for hope and happiness, marjoram for good luck, lavender for peace, and so on. You can use whatever quantity of each herb or spice you want depending on your intentions. You can even turn up the heat, if you choose, by adding cayenne pepper or mustard seed. The container that holds the herbs draws on symbolism to enhance the magic. Copper is ruled by the planet Venus, which astrologers associate with love and relationships. Red is the color of passion, and of course you know the meaning of the heart shape.

Materials Needed
- Cinnamon, stick or ground
- Dried lavender buds
- Dried marjoram leaves
- Dried oregano leaves
- Dried orange peel
- Dried rosemary sprigs
- Whole star anise
- Bowl made of copper (or a heart-shaped container of red glass or ceramic)

Steps to Take
1. Blend the herbs and spices together with your hands, using whatever amount and combination you choose.
2. While you work, envision a happy relationship that's right for you and your partner in every way.
3. Put the mixture in the bowl or container you've chosen.
4. Place the bowl in your bedroom, where you can enjoy its scent as you fall asleep.

Spell to Find Other Witches

It can be frustrating trying to connect with other witchy people. Hanging out at the local occult bookstore is one way to do it, but what if your town doesn't have one? Saint-John's-wort has been connected to witches for millennia. Saint-John's-wort is a shrubby plant with cheerful yellow flowers that is easy to identify in the wild. Harvest thin, young branches that are still flexible and bendable. Try this spell to attract other witches to you.

Materials Needed

- 3 branches fresh Saint-John's-wort
- String of twine or a thick rubber band
- Small bell with a hole or ring at the top
- 1 foot yellow ribbon

Steps to Take

Braid branches of Saint-John's-wort together while chanting this incantation (or something you write yourself):

> *"Where oh where could the wonderful witches be?*
> *"Bring me to them and them to me."*

1. Tie the ends of the braid together to make a loop or wreath, then fasten with the twine or rubber band. Tie the small bell to one end of the yellow ribbon and hang it in the center of the wreath. Use the rest of the yellow ribbon to make a loop to hang the wreath.

2. Hang your wreath near an open window or outside near your front door, knowing that every time the bell rings, it is sending out the call to other witches.

Botanical Talisman to Attract Prosperity

The botanicals in this talisman have long been prized for their abilities to attract good fortune and prosperity. Mint, for example, is hardy and grows abundantly, so it contains qualities a kitchen witch can tap in a spell for wealth. Cinnamon and cloves are mildly stimulating—they spark action in prosperity spells, but not so fast that money goes out as quickly as it comes in. (See Part 3 for the characteristics of these ingredients so you can determine how much or how little of each you want to use.)

Materials Needed

- 1 silver- or gold-colored candle in a candleholder
- Matches or lighter
- Ground cinnamon
- Whole cloves
- Dried dill
- Dried peppermint or spearmint
- Dried parsley
- Paper envelope (preferably colored silver or gold)
- 1 piece paper money (any denomination)
- Nail, knife, nail file, or other pointed tool

Steps to Take

1. Light the candle and let it burn while you work.
2. Envision your objective while you do this spell. See yourself attracting prosperity, whatever that means to you, and enjoying the fruits of your rewards.

3. Spoon some of each herb or spice, in whatever quantity you choose, into the envelope. An envelope made of silver or gold foil has the advantage of symbolizing money in virtually any culture.

4. Fold the paper bill three times, then slip it into the envelope.

5. Seal the envelope with wax dripped from the candle.

6. When the wax has partially cooled but is still soft, use the nail or other pointed tool to carve into the wax a symbol that represents prosperity to you, such as a dollar sign.

7. Put the envelope in your wallet, your purse, your desk drawer, or the cash register of your business to attract wealth.

Adjusting a Spell's Intensity How much is too much? How much is too little? You can adjust the intensity and action of a spell by adding substances that complement, calm, boost, stabilize, or speed up the energies of the other ingredients in the spell. If you're doing a botanical spell, you may want to include gemstones to augment, enhance, or offset the characteristics of the plants you've chosen. For example, if you're working a prosperity spell and you've combined herbs to spur financial growth, you might also want to add a piece of onyx, obsidian, or jet to make sure you hold on to the monetary gains you receive.

Spicy Spell for Success

This spell is intended to bring success in career or financial matters, but it can also attract recognition, achievement, or honors in other areas. You can fine-tune it to suit your purposes by adding other herbs and spices whose characteristics correspond to your objectives. (See Part 3 for information about the properties of common magical edibles.)

Materials Needed

- Ground allspice
- 1 or more dried bay leaves, whole or crumbled
- Cinnamon, stick or ground
- Mustard, seeds or powdered
- Nutmeg, whole or ground
- Tin box (or other container made of tin)
- Pen that writes gold ink
- Piece of paper

Steps to Take

1. Put a pinch (or as much as you like) of each of the spices in the tin box. Witches associate these spices with success, especially in business, career endeavors, and investments. Tin, ruled by the planet Jupiter, encourages growth and expansion.

2. With the pen, write an affirmation that expresses your goal on the paper. Gold ink brings to mind wealth as well as first-place-winning medals and awards.

3. Fold the paper three times while you state your affirmation aloud three times, then put it in the box.

4. Envision yourself receiving the success you desire and deserve. Make the visualization as rich and vivid as possible. See yourself holding a bag of gold coins, wearing a gold crown, receiving a gold medal or trophy.

5. Place the box in the public image/future gua of your kitchen (or of your home). (See the section about feng shui in Chapter 4 for more information.)

Speed Up a Spell's Action If you're in a hurry for a spell to manifest, add a little ginger, either chopped and dried or powdered. Ginger's tangy flavor kicks any spell up a notch.

Herbal Spell to Inspire Teamwork

To get business partners, coworkers, or colleagues on board with a joint project or venture, use this herbal spell to encourage cooperation. It can also help opposing parties overcome their differences and reach an agreement that benefits everyone. The main ingredient is the herb marjoram, but you can add other botanicals to fine-tune it for your purposes. For example, include peppermint or parsley for prosperity, or dill to dispel jealousy and unhealthy competition. (See Part 3 for more suggestions.)

Materials Needed

- Pink paper (pink is the color of congeniality and friendship)
- Scissors
- Pen that writes light blue ink (light blue is the color of peace and clarity)
- Small envelopes, one for each member of the team
- Dried marjoram
- Other dried herbs and spices (optional)

Steps to Take

1. Before meeting with a group of people whose cooperation you seek, cut the pink paper into strips, one for each person involved. On the paper strips, write an affirmation that expresses your intention.

2. Put some marjoram in each envelope. Add other herbs and spices if you wish (optional). Fold the strips of paper, then add one to each envelope. Seal the envelopes.

3. When you come to the negotiating table, give an envelope to each person. Tell people they can open their envelopes or not, but ask them to wait until after the meeting to do so. If tensions or arguments arise during the meeting, burn marjoram afterward to clear the air.

Botanical Banishing Spell

If harmful energies or entities (human or otherwise) are interfering with your peace and happiness, it may be time for banishing magic. This spell relies on herbs known for their properties of cleansing and protection. It also includes the element of fire, which has long been used for purification.

Materials Needed

- 1 black candle in a candleholder
- 1 white candle in a candleholder
- Matches or lighter
- Piece of white paper
- Pen that writes black ink
- Pinch dried tarragon
- Other dried protection herbs (optional)

Steps to Take

1. Set the candles in their holders on your altar or table or another work surface. Light the candles and let them burn while you work.
2. On the paper, write what you want to banish from your life.
3. Draw a circle around what you've written, then draw a diagonal line through it to signify *no*. Sprinkle a pinch of the banishing herb tarragon on the paper. You can also add other herbs, such as basil, oregano, or fennel, for additional protection.
4. Crumple the paper into a ball with the herb(s) inside. Burn the paper and herbs while you envision all disruptive energies or entities being removed from your space. Forcefully say aloud three times, "Begone, [name of whatever you are banishing]."

For Further Protection For ongoing protection, you can grow tarragon (and other banishing and protection herbs) in your garden, a window box, or containers in your kitchen.

Create a Dream Pillow

Dream pillows can help witches have magical dreams and aid in astral projection. And they can assist you in remembering your dreams. While creating this pillow, concentrate on each step to infuse the pillow with your magical power. You could also sew your stitches in patterns that feature magical numbers or symbols.

Materials Needed

- Blue thread
- Sewing needle
- 2 squares blue satin, at least 12 × 12 inches
- Sewing pins
- ½ pound cotton batting for pillow stuffing
- Handful dried mugwort

Steps to Take

1. Using the blue thread, stitch an eye on the shiny side of each piece of satin. Put the two shiny sides of the satin together.

2. Places pins on three edges of the satin to keep them in place.

3. Sew three edges of the two squares of satin together with the thread, leaving one side open, like a pocket. Keep your stitches small and close together.

4. Pull out all the pins. Turn the pocket inside out so the stitches are now on the inside and the shiny sides of the satin are now on the outside.

5. Fill the pillow halfway with cotton batting. Put a generous handful of the mugwort in on top of the cotton. Fill the pillow the rest of the way with cotton batting.

6. Stitch up the last side.

7. Place the dream pillow on your bed, under your pillow, or on your nightstand to help induce astral projection and magical dream work.

Crafting the Candles

Candle spells are probably the most popular among witches of all kinds. Candles play roles in secular and spiritual celebrations as well as in the holidays marked by people of all faiths. Kitchen witches may want to make their own candles, personalizing them for their spellwork and rituals. If you're a beginner, you may want to purchase a kit that includes all the necessary materials. Try to find a kit that uses natural soy or beeswax rather than paraffin.

When you are crafting your candles, remember to mentally project your intentions into the wax. When the candles burn, they'll release the magic power you've put into them. Also be sure to select dyes of colors that correspond to your intentions: red or pink for love, green for prosperity, black for banishing, and so on. The same goes for the containers you use. (See Chapter 4 for a list of colors and their symbolism.)

If you choose to add scent, choose essential oils whose properties support your intentions. For example:

Love	jasmine, rose, ylang-ylang, musk
Prosperity	peppermint, cedar, cinnamon, clove, vervain
Protection	pine, basil, fennel, anise
Success	cedar, cinnamon, sandalwood, patchouli
Happiness	sweet orange, bergamot
Relaxation/peace	lavender, vanilla, clary sage, chamomile

You may want to add flower petals to the wax for their aesthetic and magical characteristics. Again, select flowers whose properties align with your intentions. For example:

Love	jasmine, rose, myrtle, pink geranium
Prosperity	daffodil, marigold, tulip
Protection	carnation, lilac, white geranium, snapdragon
Success	marigold, iris, clover, violet
Happiness	daisy, orange blossom, gardenia
Relaxation/peace	lavender, chamomile, lily of the valley

Magical Candle Making

When making your own candles, you'll need some equipment, but nothing fancy. However, a warning in advance: No matter how careful you are, wax will get on everything. Wear clothes you don't mind getting wax on, and cover your surfaces with newspapers or garbage bags to keep them clean. It is also a good idea to have a dedicated set of tools to use when making candles, as it is likely you will never remove all the wax from them (so don't use your favorite wooden spoon or copper simmering pot for this project). If you buy a candle-making kit, it will have wax, wicks, and a wick-centering device (this is what the chopsticks are for).

This project involves very hot liquids. Pets and young children should be kept at a distance.

Materials Needed

- Heat-resistant glass jars (16-ounce Mason jars work well), 1 for each candle
- Candle wax (see directions in Step 2 for amount)
- Double boiler
- Silicone spatula
- 10–20 drops essential oil of your choice for each candle
- Candlewicks
- Pair of chopsticks for each candle
- Scissors

Steps to Take

1. Gather your containers. You can either use brand-new jars or, if you have old candle containers, you can repurpose them for this project. Clean them out before you start.

2. Measure out your wax. To determine how much wax you will need for each candle, simply fill your container with wax flakes or chunks up to the point that you want your candle to reach. Pour this amount into your double boiler, then do it again. The wax will condense quite a bit when melted, and it will take twice the amount of dry wax to fill the container once it is liquid.

3. Melt the wax over medium heat in your double boiler. If you don't have one, use a metal bowl set over a pot filled with water.

4. Slowly stir the wax with your spatula. This is a great moment to think about the purpose of the candle and to stir clockwise for increase or counterclockwise for decrease.

5. When the wax is completely melted, add 10–20 drops of your chosen essential oil.

6. Dip the metal end of a wick in the wax and then place it in the center of the bottom of your container. Hold it in place until the wax cools and the wick stands on its own.

7. Carefully remove the wax from the heat and pour it into your container. If your wick unsticks from the bottom, use the chopsticks laid across the top of the container to hold the wick in place (or use the wick-centering device that came with your kit if you have one).

8. Place your candle in a safe place where it will be undisturbed, and let it cool. Most candles need to sit overnight to completely harden. Once the wax is hard and completely cool, use scissors to trim the wick down to about 1/4 inch above the wax.

Candle Spell to Attract a Romantic Partner

This candle spell takes three days to perform. Three is a number witches use to seal a spell and bring it into the three-dimensional world. You'll need to leave the candles in place for that length of time, so choose a spot where they can remain safely for that period. No, they won't be burning the whole time. One candle represents you, the other symbolizes your partner.

Materials Needed

- 2 rose-colored taper candles in candleholders (if possible, use candles you've made yourself)
- Essential oil blend of jasmine, rose, ylang-ylang, and musk (or a blend that appeals to you)—you may want to mix the essential oil(s) in a carrier oil such as olive
- Matches or lighter

Steps to Take

1. Hold the candle that represents you in your hand and dress it with the essential oil blend, starting in the middle of the candle and rubbing the oil toward the tip. Don't put oil on the wick.
2. Repeat this process with the second candle, which represents your partner.
3. Position the candles 6 inches apart on your altar or in another place where they can burn safely.
4. Light both candles as you say aloud an affirmation or incantation that states your intention.
5. Let the candles burn for at least 10 minutes before snuffing them out.
6. The next day, move the candles 3 inches closer together.

7. As you state your affirmation or incantation, light both candles and let them burn for at least 10 minutes before snuffing them out.

8. On the third day, move the candles together until they are touching.

9. Repeat your affirmation or incantation as you light the candles. Let them burn down completely. (Caution: Don't leave burning candles unattended.)

10. Remove the wax stubs from their holders and melt them down. While the wax is still warm, form it into the shape of a heart.

11. Put the wax heart in your bedroom or in the relationships gua of your home (see the section about feng shui in Chapter 4 for more information).

Allow the Universe to Do Its Work Instead of doing love spells to attract a specific person, it's usually best to let the universe bring a partner who's right for you. Working magic to manipulate someone—especially if that person isn't all that interested in you—can backfire. Besides, the universe might have somebody even better for you, so don't limit yourself.

Candle Spell for Career Success
In ancient Rome and Greece, bay laurel leaves were used to crown the victors of athletic games. This spell combines the symbolism of a crown with the magical characteristics of bay leaves to help you achieve success and recognition in your career.

Materials Needed

- 1 golden or orange pillar candle (if possible, use a candle you've made yourself)
- 1 ballpoint pen
- Essential oil of cedar, cinnamon, or patchouli (carrier oil optional)
- Dessert plate, preferably white, yellow, or orange, without a design
- Dried bay leaves, enough to encircle the candle
- Matches or lighter

Steps to Take

1. Near the top of the candle, draw a crown in the wax with the ballpoint pen. The drawing should encircle the candle so it looks as if the candle is wearing a crown. It can be as simple or fancy as you choose.
2. Dress the candle with your essential oil. Don't put oil on the wick.
3. Set the candle on the dessert plate. Place the plate on the table where you eat meals.
4. Lay the bay leaves on the plate so that they encircle the candle's base.
5. Light the candle and let it burn while you eat.
6. As it burns, envision yourself achieving the success you desire and receiving the recognition, rewards, money, or other perks that you deserve.

Spell to Attract Abundance
This spell takes nine days to complete (nine is the number of fulfillment), so find a place where the materials can remain safely for that period of time. It's best to start this working on the day after the new moon. As the moon grows in light, so will your blessings. Before you begin, take some time to think about what abundance means to you. For many people, money represents abundance. Maybe good health, a loving family, and friends are also part of your abundance picture.

Materials Needed
- 9 objects that symbolize abundance to you
- 1 tray, platter, or casserole dish large enough to hold all the objects you've chosen
- 1 golden, silver, or green pillar candle big enough to burn for 90 minutes, in a glass or metal container (if possible, use a candle you've made yourself)
- Fresh mint leaves
- Fresh parsley sprigs
- Matches or lighter

Steps to Take
1. Collect the objects you've chosen to symbolize abundance.
2. In the center of the tray, platter, or casserole dish, set the candle in its container.
3. Lay some mint leaves and parsley sprigs around the candle. You will be repeating this action every day, so don't use up all the mint and parsley at once.

4. On the first day of this spell, select one of the objects you've chosen to symbolize abundance and place it on the tray, platter, or casserole dish. Say aloud a short statement of gratitude for having whatever the object represents in your life (even if it hasn't yet materialized).

5. Light the candle and let it burn for at least 10 minutes before snuffing it out. (Note: Don't leave burning candles unattended.)

6. On the second day, replace the wilted or dried mint and parsley with fresh herbs.

7. Select another of the objects you've chosen and place it on the tray, platter, or casserole dish, alongside the first item you put there. Say aloud a short statement of gratitude for having whatever the object represents in your life (even if it hasn't yet materialized).

8. Light the candle and let it burn for at least 10 minutes before snuffing it out.

9. Repeat these steps each day.

10. On the ninth day, let the candle burn down completely.

Long Weavings Some spells take days, weeks, or months to enact. They may even dip back into the past, perhaps drawing on factors from your youth, your ancestry, or previous lifetimes. These long weavings can be very powerful and have far-reaching effects. In some cases, they may involve a number of other people. Because of their scope and intensity, they can require the witch to spend time doing self-examination and preparation—mentally, emotionally, spiritually, and even physically—before beginning the magical working.

Candle Spell for Protection

This spell combines color symbolism with plant energy, aromatherapy, and the magic of the runes to safeguard your home. It's best to perform the spell on Saturday, the day ruled by Saturn, the planet of strength and endurance. In this spell you will inscribe the rune *algiz* into the candle. Ralph Blum, in *The Book of Runes*, likens this symbol to the antlers of the male elk, who uses them for protection.

Materials Needed

- 1 black candle, any size (if possible, use a candle you've made yourself)
- 1 ballpoint pen
- Essential oil of basil or pine (carrier oil optional)
- Candleholder or container for the candle
- Matches or lighter

Steps to Take

1. On the candle, inscribe the Norse rune *algiz* into the wax with the ballpoint pen. (If you prefer, you can use a nail, nail file, knife, or other sharp object.)
2. While you work, envision your home surrounded by white light.
3. Dress the candle with the essential oil and let the aroma stir feelings of strength, support, and security.
4. Place the candle in its holder or container. Set the candle on your kitchen altar, your table, or another place where it can burn safely.
5. Light the candle and let it burn while you cook or eat.

Candle Spell for Harmony and Unity

Use this spell to encourage harmony, unity, and happiness with family members or friends. It's also good for bringing a group of people together for a common purpose, shared goal, or concern that affects everyone. Choose candles of a color that represents your objective. (See Chapter 4 for more about color symbolism.)

Materials Needed

- 1 votive candle in a holder for each member of the group (if possible, use candles you've made yourself)
- Matches or lighter
- A meal to share with the group

Steps to Take

1. Set the dinner table and put a candle at each place.
2. When everyone is seated, light the candles and state aloud your joint purpose, goal, or concern.
3. Go around the table and let each person suggest ways to work toward fulfilling that objective.
4. Share the meal together, and while you eat, focus on your intention. Keep the conversation congenial and positive. Concentrate on the matter at hand, instead of bringing up other topics for discussion.
5. At the end of the meal, state together an affirmation that what you've initiated here is now manifested, with good to all concerned.

Candle Spell for Cord Cutting

A serious spell, cord cutting severs the energetic connection between two things. Witches have employed cord cutting in myriad forms. It is often utilized to separate two people after a breakup, especially if resentments or negative feelings linger. In this spell, it is best to use small candles, as both candles will need to burn down completely.

Materials Needed

- 2 small, thin candles (if possible, use candles you've made yourself)
- Matches or lighter
- Heatproof surface, like a baking sheet
- Twine (about 2 feet long)
- Salt

Steps to Take

1. Ground and center yourself.
2. Light one candle to warm the wax on top.
3. Drip a few drops of hot wax onto your heatproof surface near the middle, then press the base of your candle into the wax, anchoring it. Snuff out the candle.
4. Repeat with the second candle, placing it 3 inches away from the first.
5. Loop your twine around both candles three times. This represents the energetic ties between you. Keep the twine tight enough that it does not slide down.
6. Tie the twine somewhere between the two candles.
7. Surround the two candles with a line of salt to contain the energy.
8. Light your candles.

9. While the candles burn, say this incantation (or something that is closer to your purpose):

"I release my connection to you,
"You release your connection to me.
"Today we go our separate ways
"Like the mountains moved away from the sea."

10. Let the candles burn down. When the twine burns, this ends the connection.

11. Once the wax has cooled, throw it away.

Tea to Stimulate Career Success

Like many teas, chai is prized for its healing properties. Ginger aids digestion, cinnamon helps regulate circulation, cardamom promotes feelings of well-being, and caffeine stimulates mental clarity. Kitchen witches can use these spices for career or financial success too. Cloves and cinnamon attract prosperity, ginger brings quick results, and sugar sweetens business relationships and dealings.

Materials Needed

- 2-inch piece fresh ginger
- Wide-bladed knife
- 1 (2-quart) saucepan, copper if possible
- 15 cardamom pods
- 4 cups water
- 3 fresh cloves
- 3 teaspoons loose-leaf black tea
- Fine-mesh strainer
- Milk, to taste
- Sugar or honey, to taste (optional)
- Gound cinnamon, to taste

Steps to Take

1. Cut ginger into ½-inch-long pieces, then smash with the blade of a wide knife to release juice. Place ginger in the saucepan.
2. Smash the cardamom pods with the wide knife blade and add them to the pan.
3. Add water and bring mixture to a boil.
4. Add cloves. Simmer 10 minutes or so, then turn off burner.
5. Add black tea and let it steep 5 minutes.
6. Strain out ginger, cardamom, cloves, and tea leaves.
7. Add milk and reheat. Stir in sugar or honey if you like. Sprinkle with cinnamon for a little extra flavor and money magic. Drink this spicy tea hot or iced.

Courage Tea to Overcome Opponents

The ancients valued fennel for its medicinal benefits. In China it was considered an antidote for snake bites and insect stings, and the Greeks used it as an insect repellent. For centuries, witches have used it for protection against enemies and intruders of all kinds, human and otherwise. Contemporary kitchen witches can brew a tea from this licorice-tasting herb to boost daring, and self-confidence. Drink it when you need to beat out the competition and overcome opponents, in the boardroom or on the playing field.

Materials Needed

- 2 cups water
- 1 iron kettle (or pot)
- 1 tablespoon crushed fennel seeds
- Fine-mesh strainer
- Fresh ginger, fresh mint, lemon juice, or honey (optional, see instructions)

Steps to Take

1. Pour water into the iron kettle (or pot) and bring to a boil.
2. Add fennel seeds and simmer 10 minutes. Strain out the seeds.
3. To stimulate or speed up results, grate fresh ginger into the mix or simmer chopped ginger along with the fennel.
4. To encourage financial gains, snip fresh mint into the tea.
5. For mental clarity, squeeze in some lemon juice.
6. To sweeten a deal or win in the game of love, add a touch of honey.
7. Reheat tea and drink a cup before meeting with your opponent. Or, brew and drink fennel tea on a regular basis to boost your confidence and ward off enemies.

Moon Water

Making your own Moon Water allows you to drink the power of the moon. Also, this water is great for any spell that requires water. Just replace your plain water with Moon Water. The moon is inherently associated with water due to its influence over the tides. This technique takes advantage of color magic (see Chapter 4 for more information on color magic) and the various phases of the moon. Drink this water to cultivate a deeper relationship with the moon.

Materials Needed

- Pen that writes silver ink (silver is connected to the moon and lunar magic)
- Piece of paper
- Tape
- Glass bottle with a lid
- Water
- Window where the moon shines in

Steps to Take

1. Look up the lunar phase connected to the intentions you have for working magic and pick an appropriate night to start.
2. Using the pen, draw the lunar phase on the piece of paper and tape it to the outside of the bottle.
3. Fill your bottle with water. Close your eyes and take a few deep breaths. Concentrate on the work you intend to do with this water.
4. See the bottle and water glowing with the color associated with the work you will be doing.
5. When the time feels right, place the lid on the bottle and place it in your window. Leave the bottle in the window overnight to let the moon charge the water with its powers.

Solar–Power Chicory Coffee

Chicory is a magical botanical that is ruled by the Sun. It is used in spells to remove obstacles in your life. It's popular in the magical city of New Orleans, where it became a common coffee substitute during the Civil War and Great Depression. Drink this brew when you are in need of strength and power, or seeking a favor from a person in a position of authority. If you are cutting caffeine out of your diet, chicory is also a great coffee substitute.

Materials Needed

- 5–6 fresh chicory roots
- Sharp knife
- Baking sheet
- Coffee grinder or mortar and pestle
- French press
- Water
- Pot or kettle for boiling water
- Golden spoon (gold is the metal and color associated with the Sun)

Steps to Take

1. Cut each chicory root into nine small pieces (nine is the number of fulfillment). Spread pieces out on the baking sheet and roast in the oven at 350°F until golden brown or they start to smell like coffee (about 90 minutes).

2. Grind the roasted roots in your coffee grinder or with a mortar and pestle. Spoon the same amount as you would coffee into your French press. Boil water and pour over the grounds.

3. Stir the water and grounds clockwise nine times with a golden spoon and concentrate on success and growth.

4. Place in a sunny window and let the sun charge the mixture.

5. Drink before an important meeting or use as an ink in success spells.

Spell to Stop Gossip
No one likes to find out people are talking behind their backs. But with the proliferation of social media, texting, and a million other ways for people to communicate, gossip is not going away any time soon. This spell incorporates slippery elm, which can be found prepackaged in the tea section of your local grocery store. Yellow correlates to the planet Mercury, the element of air, and all things related to communication whether written or verbal (see Chapter 4 for more information on color magic).

Materials Needed
- Slippery elm tea
- Water
- Pot or kettle for boiling water
- Heatproof mug
- Yellow ribbon, string, or thread (9 inches long)

Steps to Take
1. Make the tea according to the directions.
2. While the tea is steeping, take your yellow ribbon, string, or thread and slowly tie nine knots in it. (Nine is the number of completion; nine knots will bring "completion" or an end to the gossip.)
3. With each knot, say out loud this enchantment (or something like it):

   "Stop talking about me unless you have my best interests in your words."

4. When you have tied all nine knots, tie the yellow ribbon around the handle of your mug.
5. Drink the tea out of your mug, occasionally repeating the enchantment.

6. When you are nearly done with the tea, untie the ribbon and drop it in the mug, allowing it to soak up the last drops.

7. When the liquid has cooled, fish out the ribbon and leave it in a window to dry in the air.

8. Once it is dry, it is now ready to work with. You can wear this ribbon like a bracelet, pin it to your pocket or bag, or store it in a safe place in any environment where you are experiencing gossip, like your workplace.

Reading Your Tea Leaves
Also called tasseography, tea-leaf reading is a divination practice that was all the rage with nineteenth-century spiritualists when tea parlors opened in America, and it became even more popular when women began opening their own tea parlors after World War I. Although it fell out of fashion for the last one hundred years or so, it is making a big comeback. To read tea leaves, you simply interpret the patterns and symbols that you see in tea leaves left in the bottom of your cup. The technique is simple, but a witch will get better at interpretation with practice. Usually it is best to use a loose-leaf black tea, drunk out of a white or light-colored cup so the leaves stand out. Whatever kind of tea you use, you need to leave some plant parts in the bottom of the cup, so tea in tea bags won't work.

Materials Needed
- Loose-leaf black tea (enough for 1 cup of tea)
- Water
- Pot or kettle for boiling water
- White teacup
- Saucer

Steps to Take
1. To start, make your cup of black tea and pour it with the leaves into the white teacup. Enjoy your tea while thinking about your question or problem.
2. Leave a little tea in the bottom of your cup, then turn the cup over on the saucer so the remaining tea drains out.
3. Tap the bottom of the cup three times.

4. After a minute or so, turn the cup back over and look at the patterns and symbols created by the tea leaves. Here are a few symbols to get you started:

Star	good luck
Ladder	travel
Circle	wedding or proposal
Apple	success
Wave	harmony
Wheel	inheritance
Crescent moon	positive changes

Blazing Hearts Hot Chocolate

Chocolate has a long-standing reputation for being an aphrodisiac. Aztecs drank chocolate in holy ceremonies and romantic interludes. It wasn't until after chocolate made its way to Spain and the court of King Charles V that it became something like the hot and sweet beverage we know today. In modern times, it is common to top a steaming mug of hot chocolate with marshmallows. Marshmallows originally got their name and flavoring from the mallow plant, which was often employed in love spells. This spell incorporates cardamom, vanilla, and oats, all sacred to Venus, the goddess of love.

Materials Needed

- 2 cups oat milk
- 2 tablespoons raw sugar
- Small saucepan
- 4 ounces bittersweet chocolate
- Red mug
- 2 or 3 marshmallows
- 2 or 3 drops vanilla extract
- Pinch ground cardamom
- Pinch ground cinnamon
- Whisk

Steps to Take

1. Heat the oat milk and sugar in a small saucepan over low heat while thinking about the warmth of love.
2. Grate or chop the chocolate into small pieces and place in your mug.
3. Cut the marshmallows into heart shapes. Set aside.
4. When the oat milk is hot, add the chocolate, vanilla, cardamom, and cinnamon to the pot. Whisk in a clockwise motion to increase love and romance in your life. As the chocolate begins to get frothy, envision a deep pink light around the saucepan. Pour the chocolate into your red mug and top with the heart-shaped marshmallows.
5. Drink or place on your altar as an offering to the power of love.

Healing Barley Water

Barley is one of the oldest grains in the world and has many healing properties. It improves gut health by reducing the amount of *Bacteroides* in the digestive system while simultaneously lowering blood sugar by boosting the amount of beneficial bacteria *Prevotella* in the gut. It is also credited with lowering cholesterol and helping with metabolism regulation. All in one little grain! It should be no surprise that magically barley is used in healing spells and spells for relieving pain and warding off negativity. Lemons cancel out negative energy and are great for lifting moods. Honey brings sweetness and blessings.

Materials Needed

- ¾ cup pearl barley
- 2 medium lemons, juiced and peeled
- Medium saucepan
- 6 cups water
- Wooden spoon
- Fine-mesh strainer
- Heatproof bowl
- ½ cup honey
- Tall glass pitcher

Steps to Take

1. Rinse the barley in cold water until the water runs clear. Envision the illness in question running down the drain.
2. Place the barley and lemon peels in a medium saucepan with the water and bring to a boil over medium heat.
3. Stir counterclockwise with a wooden spoon to encourage a reduction in sadness and negative energies.

4. Turn down the heat and simmer 15–30 minutes.

5. Strain into the heatproof bowl and set the barley and lemon peels aside.

6. Stir in the honey and lemon juice in a clockwise motion to increase health and happiness.

7. When the concoction cools, pour into the pitcher and store in the refrigerator.

8. Take the barley outside and scatter on the ground to keep evil and negativity away.

9. Compost the lemon peels, or dry them on your altar and use in spells for cleansing and purification.

10. Enjoy a glass of this whenever you're feeling down.

Witches' Brews Were Precursors to Modern Medicines Long before Big Pharma cornered the medicine market, witches created herbal concoctions to treat the sick and injured. One legendary remedy was known as "flying ointment"—made of psychotropic compounds from plants such as hemlock, nightshade, mandrake, and henbane that were toxic in high doses but, in small amounts, had anesthetic and healing properties. Today, hyoscine—a compound found in nightshade and henbane—is used for motion sickness and stomach cramps. Atropine, also found in nightshade, is a muscle relaxant and antidote to nerve gas poisoning. Willow bark was a precursor to aspirin, and the digitalis plant foxglove led to the modern drugs digoxin and digitoxin.

Bath Salts for Good Health

The Greek physician Hippocrates, known as the "father of modern medicine," believed, "The way to health is to have an aromatic bath and a scented massage every day." You can make your own bath salts to boost the power of an herbal bath. Feel free to experiment with various essential oils to discover which ones you like best and which best serve your purposes. Be sure to think positive thoughts as you work this spell, projecting them into the salt mixture.

Materials Needed

- 2 cups Himalayan pink salt, Dead Sea salt, or Epsom salt
- Large clear glass jar with a lid
- 2 drops jasmine essential oil
- 2 drops orange essential oil
- 2 drops rose essential oil
- 2 drops vanilla essential oil

Steps to Take

1. Pour the salts into the jar.
2. Add the essential oils. Cap the jar and shake it to combine.
3. Add a handful of the fragrant salts to bathwater.
4. Between baths, store the salts in a cool, dark place.

Bath to Wash Away Stress and Imbalances

Many witches take baths before engaging in rituals, ceremonies, or magic work. Not only does bathing cleanse you of energies that might interfere with your workings, it eases tension and relaxes your mind so you can open up to spiritual guidance. A ritual bath also symbolizes washing away mundane concerns as you move into the magical realm. The herb angelica, used here, is known for its ability to remove physical and psychic imbalances, leaving you ready to receive divine inspiration and direction.

Materials Needed

- Water
- Large pot
- Handful of angelica leaves
- Fine-mesh strainer
- 9 drops star anise essential oil
- 4 light blue candles
- Matches or lighter

Steps to Take

1. Bring water to a boil in a large pot.
2. Reduce heat, then add angelica leaves to the water and simmer 10 minutes. Strain out the leaves.
3. Run a bath of comfortably hot water. Pour the angelica-infused water into the bath. Add star anise essential oil to the bath.
4. Position the candles at the corners of the bathtub and light them.
5. Soak in the pleasantly scented bathwater for as long as you like. Feel tension, anxiety, and all earthly concerns slipping away. Sense your mind, body, and spirit being brought into alignment. Allow yourself to grow calm, quiet, and receptive to angelic and other spiritual guidance.
6. When you feel cleansed, cleared, and balanced, step out of the tub, extinguish the candles, and proceed with your ritual or spell casting.

Purification After Illness

Even after physically getting over a cold, you can feel run-down and depleted emotionally. Dr. Edward Bach, a homeopath who lived in the early 1900s, believed all physical illnesses had an emotional counterpart. Bathing in this herbal mix can help move some of the stagnant energies left behind after an illness.

Materials Needed

- 2 light blue candles, any size
- Matches or lighter
- Cheesecloth
- Scissors
- Dried hyssop leaves
- Dried lemon verbena
- Dried eucalyptus
- Star anise seeds
- Dried rosemary
- Blue ribbon
- Epsom salt

Steps to Take

1. Light your candles.
2. Cut a circle out of cheesecloth big enough to hold your herbs.
3. Place a handful of each herb on the cheesecloth and tie with the blue ribbon to make a sachet.
4. Run a bath with comfortably hot water.
5. Place a candle on either side of the bathtub.
6. Add a generous handful of Epsom salt to the bath. Add your prepared sachet to the water.
7. Soak in the purifying waters of this bath for a while, adding more hot water if you need to. See the illness floating away from you into the water. Let your arms and legs float in the water and feel yourself lifted up by the power of the water and purifying herbs.

8. When you feel like your energies have returned to a more natural state, get out of the bath and pull the plug.

9. See the stagnant energies accumulated in the waters swirl down the drain and out of the tub.

10. Snuff out the candles. Toss the sachet in your compost pile or scatter the ingredients in a place where they can decompose naturally. Relax and feel the restoration from this magical act.

Success Bath Bomb

Homemade bath bombs give the kitchen witch the opportunity to infuse magical intensions into every bath. Most bath bombs are spherical, but they can be molded into lots of forms, so they take advantage of shape magic.

Materials Needed

- Whisk
- ½ cup baking soda
- ¼ cup citric acid
- ⅛ cup cornstarch
- ⅛ cup Epsom salt
- Biodegradable gold glitter
- Large mixing bowl
- 2 tablespoons carrier oil, like coconut or jojoba
- ⅛ teaspoon lemon essential oil
- ⅛ teaspoon ginger essential oil
- Small bowl
- Dried lemon balm
- Plastic molds

Steps to Take

1. Whisk the baking soda, citric acid, cornstarch, Epsom salt, and gold glitter together in a large bowl until completely blended. Stir in a clockwise direction to build up the energy.
2. Pour the base oil and essential oils into the small bowl and mix clockwise until blended. Very slowly add the oil mix to the dry mix, a little at a time, whisking clockwise the whole time. Envision the mixture glowing with orange light. Focus on feelings of success and achievement.
3. When all the oil is mixed in, add just a few drops of water very quickly (the mix will fizz up a bit). You want the mixture to clump together.
4. Add the lemon balm to your molds. Then press your mixture into the molds. Leave to dry 2–4 hours.
5. Store bath bombs in an airtight container and drop one in the bath before any money-magic spell.

New Moon Ritual Bath

The new moon is a magical time to reset your energy, and it comes around once a month. Cleanse yourself and remove any old energies. This will help prepare you magically for the lunar cycle beginning at this time. Before you start, set your intentions. The new moon supports beginnings and initiates a two-week cycle of growth.

Materials Needed

- White candle
- Matches or lighter
- Lotus incense
- Calming music
- ½ cup sea salt
- ¼ cup Epsom salt
- 9 drops sandalwood essential oil
- 9 drops cucumber essential oil
- Silver (or silver-colored) cup or bowl
- Body lotion of any kind

Steps to Take

1. Light your candle. Light your incense. Start your music. Turn off the lights in the bathroom.
2. Take a few deep breaths to set your intentions for the coming month.
3. Fill the bath with water that is a comfortable temperature.
4. Add the salts and essential oils.
5. Get into the bath and visualize the moon in her dark phase, as you bathe in the dark.

6. Say your intentions for the coming month out loud, or repeat them in your head.

7. Use the silver cup or bowl to scoop up some bathwater and slowly pour it over your head three times. Visualize a silver liquid pouring over you.

8. Feel the new moon energies aligning with your physical, mental, and emotional bodies.

9. When you are done with your bath, let yourself air-dry to allow the energies to permeate your skin and energy fields.

10. Rinse the bathwater off your cup or bowl if it is metal (the salt in the bath will corrode the metal).

11. Moisturize your skin with your lotion to lock in the energies.

$3 \times 3 = 9$ Nine is a dynamic and powerful number in witchcraft. Nine is three times three—three being the number witches use to seal spells and manifest their intentions in the three-dimensional world—so that makes nine a triply powerful number in magic systems. Cats, favorite familiars for many witches, have nine lives. In many mystical traditions, nine is associated with the Goddess. In tarot, nines symbolize the perfection of a process.

Shower Meditation to Clear Your Head

Every shower can be an opportunity to wash away stress and anxiety. This spell can be enhanced with a magical shower steamer.

Materials Needed

- Shower
- A few minutes by yourself

Steps to Take

1. Turn on the shower to a comfortably hot temperature.
2. Step into the shower and let the spray hit the top of your head. Visualize all the stress and anxiety of the day like a gray film on your body. As the water runs over you, visualize that film running off your body and down the drain.
3. Concentrate on the soothing warmth and gentle massage of the water on your skin.
4. Envision the power of the water restoring you and washing away any negativity, sadness, or anxiety.
5. See yourself clean and restored, refreshed and empowered.
6. Envision your mind as a sun rising in a clear sky. Envision your mind as a field of green grass after a fresh spring rain. Envision your mind as a river full of snowmelt running strong and clear.
7. Say out loud to yourself or in your mind:

   "I can and will adapt, renew, and overcome.
   "All that holds me back is washed away."

8. When you feel clear, finish your shower as usual. Towel dry by giving yourself a vigorous rubdown and a good hug.

Venus's Beauty Bath

Beauty is in the eye of the beholder, as the old adage goes. Kitchen witches know beauty is also in the heart and mind as much as it is in looks. This spell fosters feelings of beauty in and for yourself first and foremost. If you can't get rainwater, Moon Water is a fine substitute.

Materials Needed

- Pink candle
- Matches or lighter
- Medium stainless steel bowl
- Rainwater (or Moon Water—see recipe earlier in this part)
- Fresh petals from red and white roses, divided
- Spoonful honey
- 2 cups oat milk, divided
- 13 drops jasmine essential oil
- Polished piece rose quartz
- Body lotion

Steps to Take

1. Light the candle.
2. Fill your bowl with rainwater or Moon Water. Mix in half the flower petals, a spoonful of honey, and 1 cup of oat milk. Set this bowl near the tub.
3. Run a bath at a comfortable temperature.
4. Add the jasmine essential oil to the bathwater. Add the remaining 1 cup of oat milk.
5. Toss the rest of the flower petals on the surface of the water.

6. Get in the tub and, while you are soaking, use the rose quartz to stroke the rose petal mixture in the tub on your face, arms, and legs and the rest of your body.

7. As you anoint yourself with this mixture, say this enchantment (or something you are inspired to say):

> *"Make me glow,*
> *"A shining beauty who gleams with health.*
> *"Intensify, enhance, and amplify*
> *"My inherent natural beauty."*

8. Dip your hand into the mixture in your bowl and sprinkle it over yourself and the water in the tub while laughing.

9. When you're done, get out and use some good lotion you have been saving for a special occasion.

Abundance Bath Salt Blend

This bath salt blend incorporates several prosperity elements, like green aventurine and basil, which are both aligned with wealth and abundance. Basil was folded into the sacred wraps of Egyptian mummies to spend in the afterlife. Pyrite is often called "fool's gold" because of its resemblance to real gold. Cinnamon has always been connected to wealth and was so prized in the ancient world, wars were fought over it. Napoleon Bonaparte brought silks and cashmere from Egypt that were wrapped in patchouli leaves to protect the delicate cloths from moths. While using this luxurious bath salt, think of yourself as literally soaking in a tub full of bounty and opulence.

Materials Needed

- Gold coins (real or fake)
- 1 dollar bill (or a higher denomination if you can afford it)
- 1 piece pyrite
- 1 piece green aventurine
- Green glass jar with lid
- Himalayan salt
- 1 cinnamon stick
- Dried basil
- 8 drops patchouli essential oil
- Metallic gold ribbon (long enough to go around the mouth of the jar you choose)

Steps to Take

1. Place the gold coins, dollar bill, pyrite, and green aventurine in the glass jar.
2. Add salt until the money and crystals are covered.

3. Add the cinnamon stick and basil.

4. Add more salt until the botanicals are covered.

5. Add 8 drops of patchouli oil (or less to your liking; patchouli can be strong for some people).

6. Add more salt until the jar is mostly full.

7. Place the lid on the jar and shake to combine.

8. Tie the gold ribbon around the upper part of the jar near the lid.

9. Add a heaping spoonful of the salt to any bath you take before casting money spells.

Avocado Seed Spell for Abundance

If you cut an avocado in half, you'll notice that it resembles a pregnant womb. According to sympathetic magic, this means you can use it in spells for abundance, fertility, and growth of all kinds. It's best to do this spell when the moon is waxing.

Materials Needed

- Sharp knife
- 1 medium avocado

Steps to Take

1. Cut the avocado in half. Remove the seed.
2. While the seed is still moist, carve one or more symbols that represent your intention(s) on it. This could be the rune *fehu* (possessions) or *jera* (harvest). Or, you might choose the glyph for the planet Jupiter, which astrologers connect with growth, expansion, and good fortune. A dollar sign or other symbol for currency is another possibility—whatever represents abundance to you.
3. Focus on your objective while you work.
4. When you've finished, allow the seed to dry.
5. Carry the seed with you or set it on your altar to attract the abundance you desire.
6. If you prefer, drill a hole in the seed and wear it on a cord or chain.

Poppet to Bind an Enemy's Power

A poppet is an effigy that represents a person you wish to influence in some way via magic. It can be made of any material, but this spell uses cornstalks. Fabricate it during the waning moon to limit the power of an enemy who is bent on making your life difficult. The spell won't harm the other person; it simply prevents her or him from harming you.

Materials Needed

- 1 (or more) dried cornstalk(s)
- Scissors or garden shears
- Black marker (black is the color of banishing and boundaries)
- Black cord, string, or yarn
- Tape
- Vinegar
- Spray bottle

Steps to Take

1. Using the scissors or shears, fashion a humanlike form from the cornstalk to represent your enemy. It can be any size you want it to be, even life-sized (in which case you'll need a number of cornstalks). Keep your intention in mind while you work. When you're satisfied with your creation, write the person's name on one dried leaf with the marker.

2. Tie the poppet's arms and legs with the black cord, string, or yarn, using eight knots each time. Eight is the number of permanence and banishing.

3. Tape the poppet's mouth to prevent your enemy from verbally abusing you.

4. Say aloud in a confident, commanding voice, "[person's name] you are now powerless to harm me in any way. I am safe at all times and in all situations."

5. Pour the vinegar into the spray bottle, then spritz the poppet all over with the vinegar.

6. Take the poppet to a barren place a distance away from your home and either bury it or place a large rock on it.

7. Optional: Depending on your skills and preferences, you can decorate the poppet to look like your enemy. Give it hair and facial features that are similar to your enemy's. Dress it in clothing that person might wear. It can be as simple or detailed as you want it to be.

Barley Spell to Ease Pain

Our ancestors used barley to ease physical and emotional suffering. The grain's hardiness can bring strength and endurance during difficult times too, whether you eat it or use it symbolically, as this spell does.

Materials Needed

- 3 stalks barley, fresh or dried
- 1 light blue ribbon, cord, or string made of biodegradable material

Steps to Take

1. Tie the stalks of barley together with the blue ribbon, cord, or string.
2. As you work, visually send your pain, discomfort, or unhappiness into the barley.
3. Take the barley-stalk bundle to a stream or river and toss it into the water.
4. As you watch the water whisk away the barley, feel your pain being washed away with it.

A Simple Binding Spell

Binding is a potent magical tool in a witch's arsenal and is used to shut down negative or harmful situations. Use this spell to put a stop to unhealthy activities. This should not be used to get revenge on someone you don't like or to get back at someone you feel jealousy for. Use this to remove adverse or destructive elements from a situation for the betterment of all beings involved.

Materials Needed

- White candle
- Matches or lighter
- Pen that writes black ink (black is the color of banishing and boundaries)
- Piece of paper
- Length of black thread (about 3 feet long)
- Envelope
- Cast iron cauldron or other fireproof container

Steps to Take

1. Light your candle.
2. Take three deep breaths to ground and center yourself.
3. With the pen, write a description of the problematic situation on the piece of paper. The more specific you are, the better this spell works. Stay focused on just the problem at hand.
4. When you have written all you need to, fold the paper three times.
5. Wrap the folded paper with the black thread, circling the paper nine times. Witches use the number three to seal spells and manifest them in the three-dimensional world. Because nine is three times three, it has triple power.

6. Tie the thread using nine knots.

7. Place the paper in the envelope and seal it.

8. Drip a small pool of wax on the envelope and, before it cools, scratch a binding symbol such as the rune *nauthiz* (constraint) or a sigil you've designed for this purpose into the wax or write the word *stop*.

9. Set the envelope on fire with the flame of your candle, then drop it in your cauldron or fireproof container while saying this incantation (or something similar):

"Stop this now, for the loving benefit of all beings involved."

10. When the fire completely dies out, throw the ashes outside.

Spell to Improve Psychic Abilities

Awakening and improving your psychic abilities takes time, so be patient with yourself. Use this spell to facilitate the activation of your latent psychic powers. You can utilize this spell any time you work on developing your skills. You can also make extra amounts of the botanical mixture to burn any time you work with your divination tools like tarot or runes.

Materials Needed

- Dried mugwort leaves
- Dried rosemary leaves
- Dried wormwood leaves
- Dried sage leaves
- Dried angelica flowers
- Powdered sandalwood incense
- Small dish
- Charcoal for burning incense
- Matches or lighter
- Silver heatproof container
- 1 dried bay leaf
- Book of Shadows (optional)

Steps to Take

1. Put a couple pinches each of the mugwort, rosemary, wormwood, sage, angelica, and sandalwood in your small dish and stir clockwise with your index finger until they are completely mixed.

2. While mixing your herbs, repeat this conjuration (or something similar) aloud:

   "There is a land beyond my vision.
   "Bring it into my view.
   "Show me what I have not seen.
   "Show me what I never knew."

3. Light your charcoal and place it in the heatproof container.

4. Place your bay leaf on top of the charcoal, followed by a few pinches of the dried botanical mix.

5. Repeat the conjuration while the herbs burn, watching the smoke drift up.

6. While the mixture burns, lie back with your eyes closed.

7. Envision yourself opening a book. On the pages of the book are words and images that only you can see. At first they may be blurry, but they will come into focus. You may want to write down what you've seen in your Book of Shadows.

Horn of Plenty Money Spell

The horn of plenty is a symbol of prosperity. Work this spell to bring abundance into your life.

Materials Needed

- Roll of aluminum foil
- Baking sheet
- Nonstick cooking spray
- 3 cans ready-to-bake croissants
- Olive oil

Steps to Take

1. Wad up some aluminum foil and shape it like a cone approximately 12 inches long and 6–8 inches tall.
2. Place a layer of foil around the outside to smooth it out. When you are happy with the shape, place it on its side on a baking sheet and spray the aluminum cone with a thin coat of nonstick cooking spray.
3. Pop open the cans of croissants and lay the flat triangles over the outside of the aluminum cone, making sure to overlap the edges of the dough, starting at the small end and working your way toward the larger end (pinch the edges of the triangles together if they don't want to stick).
4. As you work, envision the money in your bank accounts increasing.
5. If you have any dough left over, cut out prosperity symbols like dollar signs and stick them to the outside of the cone with some olive oil.
6. Brush the entire composition with a thin coat of olive oil.
7. Bake according to the instructions on the cans of croissants. When golden brown, take the horn out of the oven and let cool.
8. Once cool, gently remove the aluminum cone.
9. You now have an edible horn of plenty. You can stuff it with symbols of prosperity; you can eat it, taking in all that abundance magic; or you can use it as a centerpiece for Mabon celebrations.

Lucky Mojo Charm

A mojo is a lucky charm, spell, or talisman that a witch creates to attract something desired. This spell should be used to pull your goals closer. Start this spell nine days before the full moon. The last night of this spell should fall on the full moon.

Materials Needed

- Pen that writes green or gold ink
- Piece of parchment (small enough to fit in a small bottle when rolled up)
- High John the Conqueror essential oil
- White ribbon
- Small bottle with a lid
- Small piece of white cloth
- Houseplant with enough soil to bury the bottle

Steps to Take

1. Write a goal that you want to achieve on the parchment. See yourself achieving your goal. Think about how happy you will be.
2. Anoint the four corners of the parchment with the essential oil.
3. Roll up the parchment into a cylinder, like a scroll. Tie the cylinder with the white ribbon.
4. Place the cylinder in the bottle and put the lid on. Tie the whole thing up in the white cloth.
5. Place the bundle somewhere secret and safe where it will be undisturbed.

6. After three days, retrieve the bundle, open the bottle, and shake out the parchment cylinder. Hold it between your hands while you say this incantation (or something like it):

"This petition I ask to be.
"It is my heart's desire.
"Let it bring harm to none.
"Fulfillment only good will inspire."

7. Put the cylinder back in the bottle, wrap the bundle in the cloth, and hide it in your secret place again.
8. Three days later, repeat the process.
9. On the ninth day, once this spell is complete, take the bundle and bury it in a houseplant, knowing as the plant grows, so too will your achievements. Leave it to the universe to bring you into alignment with your goals when the time is right.

Call In the Experts Magic and witchcraft are powerful tools for creating change in your life, but they can only do so much. If you are having trouble with addiction or self-harm issues, use spells to assist your healing, but always seek out the advice of a trusted doctor, counselor, or therapist.

Good Decisions Talisman

Sometimes it can be hard to determine the best path through a confusing situation. And sometimes you know what is the best outcome but are tempted by solutions that are less than noble. Those tempting moments are just part of being human, but it is still your responsibility to do what is right and keep yourself on an honest and healthy path. This spell can help you make the right decisions. It uses lodestone, which is a naturally magnetized form of the stone magnetite. Lodestone was used in the first known compasses, helping people find their way.

Materials Needed

- Pen that writes black ink
- Piece of paper or parchment
- Lodestone or magnet
- Dried sage leaves
- Small bag made of red flannel that can tie shut

Steps to Take

1. Take a few deep breaths and center yourself.
2. Using the pen, write down on the piece of paper the problem you are trying to solve or question you are trying to answer. Fold the paper three times.
3. Place the lodestone or magnet, the sage, and the folded paper in the red flannel bag and tie the bag shut.
4. Place the bag on your altar to charge overnight.
5. Carry the bag with you at all times or in the situations where you feel like you may have a hard time making the right decision.
6. A solution or answer to your question should come to you within three days. It is your job to act on the advice.

Witch Bottle for Protection

Witch bottles are a very old form of spellcraft. Witches concoct them for a variety of purposes but mostly for hexing or for protection. This spell will focus on making a witch bottle for protection. Witch bottles are particularly useful in warding off magical attacks. Any negative energy sent to you will have to make its way through the bottle first.

Materials Needed

- Black candle
- Matches or lighter
- Small- to medium-sized glass bottle with a tight-fitting lid or cork stopper
- Sturdy work gloves
- Collection of sharp, rusty items like old nails, pins, and razor blades
- Sour fluid like vinegar or wine that has gone sour
- Ballpoint pen
- Shovel or hand trowel

Steps to Take

1. Light your candle.
2. *Carefully* place all the sharp things you have collected into the bottle. Wear work gloves so you don't poke yourself with any rusty metal.

3. As you fill the bottle, say this incantation (or something in the same spirit that you compose):

"Protect me and mine from the slings and arrows of my enemies,
"Turn back any ill word spoken against me,
"Turn back any evil glance cast at me,
"Break any attack thrown at me
"And send it back to the source threefold."

4. Fill your bottle with the fluid. Cap the bottle tightly.
5. Cover the lid in a thick layer of wax from your candle. Before the wax cools, draw a pentagram in the wax with the ballpoint pen.
6. Dig a hole in the ground near your front door and place the bottle in the hole. Cover it up with dirt. If it's not possible to bury the bottle in the ground, bury it in a planter near your door, or, barring that, bury it in the ground someplace where you pass by every day.
7. Snuff out the candle.

The Bottled Spell The earliest documentation of a witch bottle comes from Joseph Glanvill's 1681 book *Saducismus Triumphatus, or, Full and Plain Evidence Concerning Witches and Apparitions*. Real witch bottles have been found tucked into the foundations of houses in England, Belgium, and the United States. Their contents included hair, urine, and thorns, among other things.

Additional Resources

Websites

ANCIENT-ORIGINS.NET
Site that highlights archaeology finds, scientific research, and offers space for alternate viewpoints on those matters. Their goal is to "inspire open-minded learning about our past for the betterment of our future through research, education, and knowledge."

ATLASOBSCURA.COM
Online magazine and travel company fueled by the user-generated content of a global community of explorers, who have created a database of the world's most wondrous places as well as articles on history, science, and food.

DAVESGARDEN.COM
One of the largest sites for gardeners in the world, *Dave's Garden* features tens of thousands of encyclopedic files on plants, bugs, and birds, as well as helpful articles by gardening experts.

FlyingtheHedge.com

Blog by hedge witch Autumn Willow that features, among other things, an A-to-Z guide of magical herbs and their uses.

GaiaHerbs.com

Website for the Gaia Herbs company and their extensive line of herbal supplement products.

GardenersPath.com

Gardening advice such as planting tips, fixes for common problems, and reviews of gardening products, tools, and supplies.

HerbalGram.org

Website of the American Botanical Council (ABC). The ABC's goal is to provide accurate and reliable information and education on the safe and effective use of herbal medicine.

LearnReligions.com

Website dedicated to educating people on the major faiths and religions of the world. Features articles written by ministers, authors, licensed clergy, and teachers.

Magic-Spells-and-Potions.com

Sample spells and rituals for the beginner practitioner, constructed by StarFields.

MoodyMoons.com

Online community that features ritual ideas, crafts, recipes, beauty spells, witchy travel destinations, and more for the modern witch.

PAGANPAGES.ORG

Online magazine featuring articles on recipes, crafts, celebrating holidays, and mindful living; interviews with authors and prominent practitioners in the field; and book and card deck reviews.

PATHEOS.COM

Web platform featuring articles and a library on the religions of the world compiled by top religious leaders and scholars. Articles in the religious categories cover topics such as current events, philosophy, history, and more.

PLENTIFULEARTH.COM

Website for a metaphysical supply and spiritual shop based in Austin, Texas, that features products to buy and also free content such as spells, recipes, and a spiritual blog.

THECONVERSATION.COM

Nonprofit, independent news website featuring articles written by academic experts on topics such as policy, science, health, economics, education, history, ethics, and more.

THEDRUIDSGARDEN.COM

Website of the current grand archdruid of the Ancient Order of Druids in America. Features writings, artwork, and teachings.

WITCHESANDPAGANS.COM

Website for *Witches&Pagans* magazine, which focuses on covering contemporary pagan culture, as well as interviews and visits to sacred places.

WITCHESOFTHECRAFT.COM

Blog and informational website from Lady Carla Beltane, which includes information on spells, sabbats, crystals, and herbs, among other things.

WITCHIPEDIA.COM
An online encyclopedia of witchcraft, magic, and the occult.

WITCHYGYPSYMOMMA.COM
Website for kitchen witch Laurie. Includes a large herbal library for reference and a shop to purchase her herbal blends and salves.

Books

The Book of Runes, 25th Anniversary Edition by Ralph Blum. Thomas Dunne Books, 2008.

Find Your Goddess: How to Manifest the Power and Wisdom of the Ancient Goddesses in Your Everyday Life by Skye Alexander. Adams Media, 2018.

The Green Witch: Your Complete Guide to the Natural Magic of Herbs, Flowers, Essential Oils, and More by Arin Murphy-Hiscock. Adams Media, 2017.

The House Witch: Your Complete Guide to Creating a Magical Space with Rituals and Spells for Hearth and Home by Arin Murphy-Hiscock. Adams Media, 2018.

Magickal Astrology: Use the Power of the Planets to Create an Enchanted Life by Skye Alexander. Red Wheel/Weiser, 2019.

The Modern Guide to Witchcraft: Your Complete Guide to Witches, Covens, and Spells by Skye Alexander. Adams Media, 2014.

The Modern Witchcraft Spell Book: Your Complete Guide to Crafting and Casting Spells by Skye Alexander. Adams Media, 2015.

The Rulership Book by Rex Bills and Kris Brandt Riske. American Federation of Astrologers, 2007.

Index

About the Author

Skye Alexander is the award-winning author of nearly fifty fiction and nonfiction books, including *Your Goddess Year, The Only Tarot Book You'll Ever Need, The Modern Guide to Witchcraft, The Modern Witchcraft Spell Book, The Modern Witchcraft Grimoire, The Modern Witchcraft Book of Tarot,* and *The Modern Witchcraft Book of Love Spells.* Her stories have been published in anthologies internationally, and her work has been translated into more than a dozen languages. The Discovery Channel featured her doing a ritual at Stonehenge in the TV special *Secret Stonehenge.* She lives in Texas.

"The Green Witch *is a delightful guide to nature magic. It's filled with practical recipes for herbal blends and potions, the properties of essential oils, and lots of ideas for healing and relaxation.*"
—BUSTLE

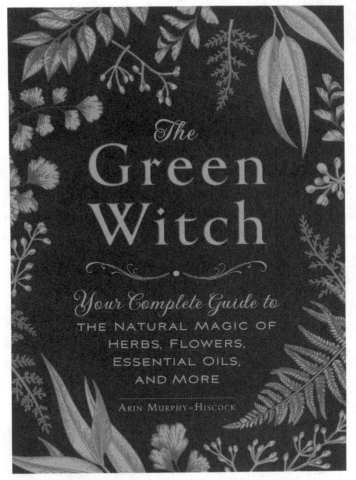

PICK UP OR DOWNLOAD YOUR COPY TODAY!